VINCENT D'INDY

VINCENT D'INDY
1851—1931

Vincent d'Indy
1851-1931
CHAMPION OF CLASSICISM

A study by
NORMAN DEMUTH
Hon. R.A.M., Hon. A.R.C.M.
Officier d'Académie

Professor of Composition,
Royal Academy of Music, London

SALISBURY SQUARE LONDON

Made and printed in Great Britain by
The Central Press (Aberdeen), Limited

FOREWORD

THIS is a tribute to a very great musician on the occasion of the centenary anniversary of his birth. In it I have endeavoured to present pictures of Vincent d'Indy as a man, a teacher, and a composer. I have placed the sections in this order because his work in the last-named capacity underlines that in the second; I do not suggest that he was greater as a teacher than as a composer, because his quality was the same in both. I have told elsewhere[1] of the circumstances in which I first came into contact with d'Indy himself and his works, the former contact coming, alas, much too near his death to be of any benefit to me. It has been a matter of deepest regret that circumstances prevented me from becoming a Schola Cantorum student after the 1914-18 War.

The scope of this little book does not permit any detailed biographical section, and I have been compelled to restrict such information to those places where it coincides with some particular work. It should be remarked here, however, that d'Indy lived through one of the most interesting periods in the history of music. He knew, personally, Rossini, Meyerbeer, Wagner, Liszt, Brahms, Franck and other musicians of historical and musical importance. The only one to have eluded him was Berlioz; there is no reference in his letters or writings which shows any interest in or experience of Berlioz' music while that composer was alive.

Such factual points as have been essential have been collated from the French sources quoted in the Bibliography. I have benefited in this respect from a long conversation with

[1] *Music Survey*, Vol. III, No. 3.

the late Pierre de Bréville (1861-1949) during the summer of the year of his death. M. de Bréville was not only a fellow-student with d'Indy (of Franck), but was entrusted with the completion of any unfinished works left by d'Indy, this instruction being contained in the composer's " testament artistique ".   M. Guy Ropartz, also a fellow-student of d'Indy, and M. Guy de Lioncourt, d'Indy's nephew and Director of the Ecole César Franck, have from time to time answered many questions I have asked and have volunteered much interesting and valuable personal information, the former during my preparation of my book on Franck and the latter during that of the present book, particularly by sending me issues of the *Tablettes de la Schola* and the *Bulletins de l'Ecole César Franck*.   I am deeply grateful to these two musicians for the immense pains they have taken to give me the information I have required.

I have not attempted full analyses of all the works or, indeed, of very many of them.   d'Indy not being a familiar name on our concert programmes as yet, I have thought it better to give a broad and general outline of his work which will, I hope, not only arouse the interest of the reader, but will afford a fair panorama of d'Indy's ideals, musician-ship and technique.   I am encouraged in the thought that the interest in d'Indy is steadily growing, if it is possible to judge from the correspondence I have had with numbers of English musicians and societies by virtue of being the " delegué pour l'Angleterre " of the " Comité d'Action " organising the anniversary celebrations, and the practical intentions of my correspondents cause me to think that there is a very real chance of d'Indy coming into his own here.

The purpose of this book, therefore, is two-fold; one, to offer tribute and homage, and, two, to tell the student and music-lover something about the riches which are to be found in the music of Vincent d'Indy.

Bognor Regis,   NORMAN DEMUTH.
Christmass Day, 1950.

CONTENTS

ACKNOWLEDGEMENTS

As usual, I must thank my wife for all her unstinted assistance in reading typescript and proofs, and the several friends in Paris who have given me their personal knowledge of d'Indy and have told me something of his methods of work, etc.

The publishers owning the copyrights in the music have once again generously allowed me to quote from the scores to illustrate points in the context, and to them I tender my most grateful appreciation of their co-operation. The publishers in question are:

MM. DURAND ET CIE

> Piano Sonata
> Violin Sonata
> "Jour d'Eté à la Montagne"
> Symphony in B flat
> Second String Quartet
> " Istar " Variations
> " Fervaal "
> " L'Etranger "

MM. HAMELLE ET CIE

> Symphonie Cévenole

MM. HENN ET CIE (GENEVA)

> Treize Pièces Brêves

MM. ROUART LEROLLE ET CIE

> Concerto for Piano, Flute, 'Cello and Strings
> " La Légende de Saint-Christophe."

CHAPTER ONE

The Man

VINCENT D'INDY was an aristocrat by birth, coming from a noble sixteenth-century family. From the time of Henri IV all the members played important rôles in French history; but the arts of peace were also practised from generation to generation, and the composer had two uncles, Wilfrid and Antonin, who were both cultivated musicians. The former composed several chamber and theatre works which enjoyed some vogue. The latter, a pupil of Zimmerman for piano, was a frequent *habitué* of musical parties and moved in high Parisian circles. He was an intimate friend of Hector Berlioz and had the *entrée* to Berlioz' house. These two uncles were midway between professional and amateur musicians. They viewed music as more than a pastime and took it seriously enough to make a regular study of it. On the other hand, they were not musicians by calling, and the management of their respective estates and other affairs required their prior attention.

d'Indy was brought up by his grandmother, the Comtesse Rezia d'Indy, and the almost tyrannical discipline under which he spent his boyhood and youth left its mark upon his personality and method of work. Within a small circle coincidences are of frequent occurrence, but it may be remarked that when the Comtesse subscribed to some Trios composed by a certain rather obscure composer named César Franck, she little guessed the important rôle that that composer was to play in the life of her grandson. The

1

Comtesse was not anxious that her grandson should follow in the family military tradition, but when d'Indy unexpectedly turned up one day during the Franco-Prussian War in soldier's uniform, her pride knew no bounds. This was increased when he took part in the actual fighting and came to close grips with the Germans in several bayonet charges (neither d'Indy nor any other French composer feared that serving " la patrie " would injure musical sensitivity).

d'Indy's remarkable attention to small details may be ascribed to the circumstances of his early life, during which his mind was cultivated and became so well-ordered as to threaten disaster in the face of the slightest dislocation. d'Indy, however, was a Frenchman and lacked that literal approach to life which precludes quick thinking and adjustment when organisation breaks down. Clarity of mind in any emergency is essential, and this well-ordering of d'Indy's impressionable years served him well in his musical symphonic researches, and endowed him with magnificent powers of organisation in everything he undertook. He learned to take responsibility and act upon his own initiative, for the Comtesse never repressed.

d'Indy's home in the Rue du Bac was a model of precision and exactitude, and he lived to a strict time-table which was never relaxed. He was gregarious and had many friends of his own age who were not in the least awed by the châtelaine of the house. They were allowed to make as much noise as they liked and in every way behaved as normal children (I emphasise this, as certain passages in M. Léon Vallas' book suggest that d'Indy may have been a little prig).

His youthful passion was for toy soldiers, a passion shared by boys everywhere; but there was none of that haphazard arrangement of battles which characterise the average toy-soldier campaign. d'Indy organised his model forces with true military precision and authority. That his army invariably won the day was due both to his instinctive skill in military tactics and deployment, and to the fact that he constituted himself the leader in every game, no matter what it may have been, and leaders invariably get their own way. His favourite historical character was Napoleon Bonaparte, and all d'Indy's toy battles were fought upon the actual strategy of the Emperor's big European battles. This early passion was naturally squeezed out of his life when he became a musician, but the power of organisation and his remarkable memory never failed him. In proof of this, we may quote two visits to the battlefield of Waterloo in 1865 and 1897. On the former occasion he indicated the exact positions of the forces as he had studied them in books, and he ranged through the whole battle in this way. On the latter he astonished his son, then a Lieutenant of Dragoons, by reconstituting the events in their most minute details, doing so with the skill and authority of a great tactician.

Further evidence of this remarkable attention to detail can be seen in his habit of carefully dating every section of any work upon which he was engaged.

This naturally led to enthusiasms which knew no bounds. d'Indy was not content simply to carry out some undertaking; he had to go further. It was not enough for him that he should merely serve in the 105e Bataillon de la Garde Nationale de Paris during the Franco-Prussian War; he had to write the history of that battalion. This thoroughness stayed with him all his life. Having a passion for travel (and the means with which to gratify it), he walked home from Switzerland to Paris on one occasion, deeming that in this way he would see more of the country than otherwise. Those who know Paris may visualise the distance between the Avenue de Villars, near the Invalides, and the Rue St. Jacques, near the Panthéon. d'Indy walked that distance every day, in both directions, and he did it slowly and with dignity—for in all circumstances d'Indy was innately dignified, whether he was at a reception or taking the place of a

missing triangle-player at an orchestral concert; and this
dignity was never in question. Not even a shell from " Big
Bertha " bursting within a few yards of him disturbed
his equanimity; he merely made notes of the distance and
the circumference of the shell-hole, which he calculated
accurately with a single glance, and passed on his way.
This dignity, however, gained for him a reputation of
frigidity and aloofness which, once they had been penetrated,
were found to be not really part of his nature; but he rarely
allowed himself the joy and pleasure of real verbal exultation.
This he confined to his letters, and here he was as
indefatigable as any Georgian. His spidery handwriting may
have been legible to those who knew it, but the initiation was
a long process. The words flow in easy and spontaneous
succession, not only across the page, but from the bottom of
the margin, upwards, and there is very little space left bare
of them. He took infinite pains, no matter how small the
question he had to deal with. His powers of reasoning
were astonishing, but they were sometimes marred by rather
a pig-headed obstinacy. He stuck to his guns and proved his
strength of mind; and not even the acid and disillusioned
Camille Saint-Saëns, who from being one of his closest
friends became one of his bitterest opponents, could deny
him the quality of sincerity.

His powers of organisation reveal themselves in his logical
symphonic processes which are impeccable and completely
irrefutable. From this point of view there can be no adverse
criticism, but it will be apparent during the study of the
music that his passion for musical form superficially appears
to have taken precedence over musical feeling, although he
strenuously maintained that the ideas must dictate the form,
not the form the ideas. His mental organisation impressed
upon his musicality the necessity for tonality and key relationship upon a polyphonic basis. Although as a student he
hated counterpoint, he was a strenuous advocate of it for
the formation of a natural technique. He prescribed so

rigid a course of training for his pupils that some were unable to sustain it, and, while maintaining the greatness of d'Indy himself, refused to submit their backs to the technical scorpions considered right and proper for them.

Another reflection of d'Indy's early disciplinary training may be found in his businesslike capacity for the ordering of ordinary matters. When, in 1876, he was appointed Secretary of the Société nationale, he found everything in a state of glorious disorder. Minutes of meetings had been scribbled down in pencil quite haphazardly, and no attempt had been made to preserve complete records of activities. Within a very short time d'Indy had collected details of previous concerts, etc., and had carefully tabulated them. Henceforth, the Minutes were recorded almost verbatim, many sheets of paper being covered in the process, while reviews and criticisms were carefully filed. Reading these Press notices confirmed d'Indy in the opinion quoted on page 46.

His was an unquestioning and consummate Faith and upon that rock he built the edifice of his life. M. Romain Rolland[1] envisaged him burning heretics with zeal (and possibly pleasure), but this faith was more than an academic adherence to the tenets of Christianity; in his eyes, it was the only way of life. One reads and hears of no pettiness and backbiting on his part, for he viewed his opponents with sympathy rather than with anger.

Nevertheless, he was human and was possessed of a sense of humour allowed only rarely to come to the surface, and then only amongst his intimates. Cynical he undoubtedly was: when asked about a pause usually made by sopranos in an aria from *Der Freischütz*, he replied that its length depended upon whether the singer were the mistress of the conductor or not. He noted with some pleasantry that Meyerbeer's successes had always coincided with epidemics of cholera! This humour is read at its best in his final

---

[1] *Musiciens d'Aujourd'hui.*

volume of the *Cours de Composition musicale*, which does not hesitate at indicating operatic absurdities of a detailed nature which usually escape the commentator and writer upon opera.

He was intolerant only of what he considered false doctrine, and would not stand humbug for a single moment. He was not alone in regarding Schoenberg as a " madman " at the time of that composer's systematic doctrinisation, and he did not appreciate the " new thought " of Les Six; but he did not condemn it whole-heartedly or in a wholesale manner, for he was inclined to the opinion that the great young man of the period was Arthur Honegger. When asked, d'Indy replied that music would go in whatever direction the next composer of genius took it.

This sincerity for Art (which he always spelt with a capital "A") may have been caused partly by the fact that he adopted it as a career and calling with no encouragement from his family. Indeed, his father threatened to cut him off with the proverbial shilling, but d'Indy had inherited his grandmother's fortune, so that the paternal dismissal would have made but little difference to him; and here we come to the astonishing phenomenon of his dual personality. He was torn in two directions. Fundamentally he was the aristocrat, underlined by his personal appearance. Instinctively he held other people in disdain, but he cured himself of this by associating, not with the conductor's rostrum, but with the back desks and background instrumentalists, particularly the percussion players. He knew that in order to learn his craft he should make personal contact with the actual craftsmen. Meticulously he drew up lists of all those players with whom he was acquainted. Avidly he listened to everything they had to say. Persistently he asked question after question—and even in those troublous times of social revolution, when everything d'Indy stood for was anathema, he succeeded in directing attention away from his background and on to his particular *métier*. He knew how difficult orchestral players can be when they set their minds to it, and his personal knowledge of them enabled him to place the violence of their actions and the rudeness of their words in their true perspective. It was some while before he accustomed himself to the realisation that not all of them were as full of their mission in life through Art as he was himself. However, he never refrained from doing himself everything he expected from others. He was happy to stand down from the conductor's rostrum and take up a tambourine in the orchestra if no player were available, or to stand in the *coulisses* night after night at the Opéra-Comique in order to give a singer his note (this he did for Bizet's *Carmen*). Nothing was too small for him to undertake in the cause of his beloved Art.

His great ambition was to be a musician and an artist. Consequently he went to extraordinary lengths in order to place himself naturally in the proper surroundings and atmosphere. He would copy band parts if necessary, realising that this work would give him a rare insight into scoring. He never took advantage of his private resources and would eat in the humble restaurants rather than in those to which these resources would have permitted. Léon Vallas tells a story of the astonishment shown by one of his closest friends when, after months of economical living, he discovered that d'Indy was a man of means. d'Indy was thus able to adjust himself to the reduced circumstances in which he, with countless others, found himself after the First Great War.

Endowed with almost superhuman energy, he did not know what it was to be tired. After a strenuous day at the Conservatoire or Schola Cantorum, he was perfectly willing to spend the rest of the evening on his own work or would catch a train to some outlandish spot to lecture or take a rehearsal; and he was up betimes each morning. The late Pierre de Bréville told me that Franck sent him to study orchestration with d'Indy—" He knows more about it than

I do "—and d'Indy suggested that he should come for his first lesson at—5 a.m.; and this was neither affectation nor a method of ridding himself of an onerous job, which, of course, it was not.

This energy never forsook him. The year before his death the writer saw him conduct a performance of a concert version of *La Légende de St. Christophe* at the Salle Pleyel, given by the students of the Schola Cantorum. The clarity of his beat, the determination with which he directed the work to climax after climax and, above all, the affection with which he was received by performers and audience, made this memorable. In 1914 he was disgusted because the Government would not let him enlist once more in the French Army, and he assured the Minister for War that his legs were much stronger than those of many younger men. He visited his son not far from the firing line, and while in Paris would go out of his way to talk to any stray soldier he might see in a *bistro*, no matter how humble, and thus learn at first hand the experiences of a twentieth-century war. His theory was that since the soldiers had but little protection and were unable to run away, the civilian population should live under the same conditions. A professor who suggested that the Schola should be evacuated or should at least take shelter during the time of bombardment was promptly dismissed. Blanche Selva was hard put to it to find a reason for over-staying her holiday, while a mother who suggested removing her daughter from the Schola until the end of the War was told that if she did this, the daughter could stay away for good. One must remember that the circumstances of 1914-1918 were not as severe, save in proportion, as those in 1939-1945. d'Indy, however, would have been a sore trial to Air Raid Wardens, but what a warden he would have made! He was by this time infinitely approachable by all and sundry; but he was not in the least democratic, and the ease of approach which he cultivated within himself was not achieved without some difficulty and internal struggle, and was attended by considerable restraint at times.

He was a loyal friend and never allowed himself to be influenced by personal feeling. This was probably innate, but he received his lead from his beloved Franck, whose musical disappointments were innumerable. His loyalty, however, caused him to exaggerate and even dramatise situations at times. His reverence for Franck almost passed the bounds of reason. With the best will in the world, d'Indy, in his book on Franck, gives an overdrawn picture of the saintliness and mysticism of the man. Readers of this book are led to believe that Franck was a bigot and one far too pure for this earth. The fact, as I have explained with the full authority of MM. Pierre de Bréville and J. Guy Ropartz (his pupils),[1] was that Franck was an essentially good man and, in a world where such goodness played a very small part, this element stood out in bold relief. No one can blame d'Indy. One invariably has a highly coloured picture of one's idols, and it so happens that d'Indy's picture of Franck was rather too roseate in hue.

Outwardly, d'Indy had the air of the *grand seigneur*. Inwardly, he was not only a passionate and sincere creative artist, filled with the highest ideals, but a veritable *grand maître*. This duality of birth and profession he shared with Marie de Saint-Victor Alexis, Vicomte de Castillon (1838-1873), who died prematurely after giving evidence of obvious musical genius. Not even Paul Dukas himself, a man of consummate dignity, can be considered a parallel with d'Indy in his capacity of *grand maître*.

At the rostrum, d'Indy always paused before actually giving the opening beat, as if summoning up before him the spirits of the great composers of the past whose music he was about to conduct. When it was a modern work, he adopted a similar attitude, and one could be sure that it was a short prayer that he was uttering, asking that he should be given

[1] *César Franck, op. cit.*

2

full strength to carry out the high artistic duty which lay before him. All this may seem a trifle stifling, a little too high-
minded and possibly lacking in a sense of humour; but it was
d'Indy himself, and those who knew him at work say that
he carried to this work the element of good nature and kindly
humour, which, nevertheless, was never allowed to get out of
hand. One may perhaps compare his attitude and methods
with another Bach-lover, one who was not a composer, who
was to a certain extent eccentric and had equally high ideals.
It is reported of Sir Hugh Allen (1869-1946)[1] that he once
told a choir very seriously when rehearsing a work of J. S.
Bach " When you sing it up there, don't forget that it will
be J. S. B. who will be conducting." d'Indy could never
have put it quite that way, but in all surety he communed
silently and quickly with " J. S. B." before conducting the
Mass in B minor or the *Passions*, but he could never have
thought of him in those terms.

He was companionable and slow to anger, but when
roused, as furious as any lion. Nothing upset him more than
a singer taking liberties; but the remark of a student that the
intricate lines of notes he had written were " visual counterpoint " roused his ire to an undreamed-of pitch. Bidding the
student come up to a picture, he asked him to listen to it,
saying that it was an " aural painting ". The explosion of
wrath and cynical sarcasm which then followed completely
shattered the misguided student. However, in all this he
was dignified, and those who suffered his ire realised that it
was aroused solely by his passionate sincerity for Art.

The picture which one has of him times itself at the hour
in the morning when Paris is about to wake up. The
dignified figure of Vincent d'Indy, erect, in Inverness-type of
overcoat if in the winter, walking-stick in hand, cigarette in
long holder, proceeds either to the Conservatoire or to the
Schola Cantorum, greeting the multitude of street-cleaners,
postmen, milkmen, etc., with a courteous word or inclination

[1] *Hugh Allen*, H. C. Colles (O.U.P.).

of the head, for all the world like a retired colonel out for a morning stroll and not in the least like one to whom the principles of Art were veritable ideals, and giving little indication that beneath that façade there beat the kindest of hearts. Thus he represented the direct antithesis to the traditional " artist " of Murger and Montmartre. It is doubtful if he ever relaxed. Certainly he had no hobbies like the kite-flying and chemistry practised by Elgar, whom, to a certain extent, he suggests. The spirituality of the two composers was similar, but while nothing would induce Elgar to talk about music, nothing except military strategy would prevent d'Indy from so doing. With certain reservations, d'Indy may be paralleled with Elgar (of the Symphonies and Concertos, and the *Introduction and Allegro*—not he of *Pomp and Circumstance*) as a composer; with Parry as a man (but without Parry's excessive and violent geniality); and with Stanford and Tovey (particularly the latter) as a teacher.

d'Indy died suddenly, while at work on his book on Wagner. Thus he joined the small body of musicians who died in full harness—Girard, who collapsed suddenly immediately after conducting a performance of " Les Huguenots ", Ernest Guiraud who dropped dead while addressing a conference at the Paris Conservatoire, and Louis Vierne whose end came just after he had played the last chord in an organ recital at Notre-Dame, in Paris—lives all fully and truly completed in the cause of Art.

He received honours, decorations and awards from America and nearly all European countries, excluding ours. It did not occur to any of our institutions or universities to honour him with an honorary degree, fellowship or membership. As Commander of the Legion of Honour, d'Indy was given a military funeral with all honours. However, in the words of the writer in the Funeral Number of *Les Tablettes de la Schola*, it was neither this panoply nor the crowds of people who walked in the procession and lined the streets which made the deepest impression. It was the tears of the young students who followed the bier and crowded round the grave which made the occasion one to be ever remembered.

"At his death, a very old man is often regretted; he is rarely mourned by any save his nearest, and by those of his own generation. The *Maître*, dying in his eighty-first year, was mourned as if he had been a young man cut off in the flower of his youth, as if he had been a child, a wife, or a mother. The Schola, on that fifth of December, witnessed the moving spectacle of a crowd of young people in tears before the bier of an octogenarian."

This, surely, is sufficient denial of d'Indy's reputed severity, segregariousness, and frigidity.

CHAPTER TWO

The Teacher

THE initial impulse to put forward a system in opposition to the prevailing principles of the Paris Conservatoire came from the particular method of instruction which d'Indy received at the hands of César Franck. The story of the " Franck Family " has been told in many places and need not be repeated here.[1] It will suffice to say that while Franck based his teaching upon the example of the established masters, particularly the later Beethoven, the Conservatoire focussed attention upon Opera of a highly stylised nature and the Prix de Rome (which, incidentally, d'Indy did not win). The idea of what was to be d'Indy's monumental *Cours de Composition musicale* came to him in 1875 when he attended some of Liszt's Piano Classes in Weimar. The plan was put into operation through collaboration in another direction.

In 1890 Charles Bordes (1863-1909) was appointed *maître de chapelle* at Saint-Gervais and at once opened a campaign for the revival of Palestrina and other then unknown polyphonic composers. In 1891 Bordes performed the *Miserere* of Allegri and the *Stabat Mater* of Palestrina. The following year he continued the revelation of music which had hitherto lain in libraries unsung, by devoting the whole of Holy Week to polyphonic and Gregorian music, soliciting the aid of d'Indy in this enormous undertaking. The singers were willing, but incapable of appreciating the flattened seventh of Gregorian music for some while. The same year Bordes

[1] The reader will find this, and the general musical situation in Paris, dealt with fully in my *César Franck* (Dennis Dobson).

13

and d'Indy founded the " Société des Chanteurs de Saint-Gervais " and in 1894 gave the first of an unprecedented series of annual performances of Bach's Cantatas. They were joined in this venture by Alexandre Guilmant (1837-1911). From this beginning there appeared an *Anthologie des maîtres religieux primitifs* which caused some sensation since the music was completely unknown at the time. The "Chanteurs de Saint-Gervais" became so popular that Bordes decided to form them into a regular organisation, and, with the collaboration of d'Indy and Guilmant, formed the " Société Schola Cantorum ", which also in 1894 published the first number of a periodical entitled *La Tribune de Saint-Gervais*. Here the four principles of the " Société Schola Cantorum " were put forward, the most important being the return to Gregorian tradition in the performance of plain-song, the establishing of Palestrina and his School as the model for all church music, and the creation of a modern church style founded upon the technique of Palestrina.

Eventually, in 1896, there was founded the now well-known Schola Cantorum. For that moment it was devoted entirely to church music and may be likened to our present School of English Church Music. The scope was extended to counterpoint and composition under d'Indy, organ under Guilmant, solfège and *classe de clavier*. Bordes worked indefatigably. The enterprise was started with the princely capital of 37 francs 50 centimes—such is Faith. The activities of the newly-founded institution were extended to the provinces, and the Paris headquarters took on the further responsibility of a choir school. It is needless here to go into the complete working of the association, and it will be enough to state that the complete revival of church music emanated therefrom and received the approbation of the highest dignitaries of the Roman Catholic Church. Among the many activities which should be mentioned, however, was that of Bordes, who took over a model of the church of Saint-Julien des Ménétriers au Vieux-Paris which had been erected in the middle of the Exhibition of 1900. There Bordes organised twenty-minute musical performances between the hours of three o'clock and six o'clock every day, with a fifteen-minute interval between each. It was estimated that 60,000 people in all attended these " concerts spirituels ". However, a still greater expansion followed. In 1900 the Schola Cantorum moved to premises in the Rue Saint-Jacques, a building which had been used for widely differing purposes during the course of its history, acting as the headquarters of the expelled English Jesuits who came over with James II and, during the Revolution, a prison. It was agreed that the scheme should no longer be restricted to church music but should be widened to bring it within the scope of an ordinary general conservatoire of music. d'Indy became Director, while Bordes undertook the propaganda side of the affair. On 2 November 1900 Vincent d'Indy gave the inaugural address, explaining the policy which would direct the programme.

d'Indy thus found that one of the ambitions of his life was achieved. He was the head of a Conservatoire and the whole instructional policy lay within his hands and under his responsibility. It is not accurate to say that he actually *founded* the Schola Cantorum, but it is perfectly right to regard him as the founder of the institution as it is known to-day.[1]

d'Indy's address caused a sensation; nothing so direct had ever been heard before in connection with the directional policy of a teaching institution. He commenced by declaring that since Art was not a craft, no school of Art should be an institution for turning out professionals. This was a shaft aimed directly at the Conservatoire. d'Indy made no secret of the fact that the teaching at the Schola Cantorum would follow the lines of that of César Franck, and that the friendly feeling which characterised the " Franck Family " would

[1] The reader's attention is directed forward to page 19.

be encouraged. He made it plain that it was his determination to work along the broadest principles and in this way make the students fully aware of musical technique and history outside the narrow realm of their own instruments. He instanced several cases of narrow-mindedness and ignorance on the part of both professors and students at the Paris Conservatoire. He would have none of the attitude admitted by Adolphe Adam (1803-1856), who said that he got no joy out of music or of composing it, and that he wrote it because he could do nothing else. This approach to Art would never exist within the walls of the Schola Cantorum. Another case quoted was that of the Prix de Rome winner who, hearing the " allegretto " from Beethoven's Seventh Symphony for the first time, exclaimed during the opening bars, " That is pretty; it might have been written by Saint-Saëns ". This ignorance, d'Indy explained, was due entirely to the literal nature of the training which dealt with the matter in hand and did not allow any enquiry further afield. He pointed out the danger of this policy, since students left the Conservatoire with little knowledge or experience of the works of the great composers outside their own particular subject, while within it their knowledge was restricted to the actual works they were studying. In other words, the Schola Cantorum would not turn out mere instrumentalists interested only in their own instruments, and in the music they themselves made.

Franck had always made a point of referring to the established composers for authoritative confirmation of what he said, and the Schola training was to work upon this basis. While there would be the normal classes for technique and basic training, once these classes had been finished with, the student would immediately enter upon a practical and historical study of form and composition. d'Indy stated that since it was necessary for a violinist, for example, to be able to play a Corelli Sonata and be fully aware of its shape and outline, so was it equally necessary for a composer to know all about the earliest examples of musical composition, for without a thorough knowledge of his subject from its earliest sources, he could not be expected to know how to set about ordering his musical thoughts and ideas. Before embarking upon an original sonata or symphony he must be able to start from the beginning and progress along the paths as followed by composers all through the history of music. He considered it no more feasible that a first-year composer should write a full-length modern symphony than that a first-year instrumentalist should start with a Beethoven or Brahms Sonata. Free discussion was to be encouraged and every novel technique examined for all its latent possibilities before being either accepted or discarded.

In this harangue d'Indy left nothing to the imagination. He put forward his ideals with the utmost frankness, making it perfectly obvious that nobody need expect to be directed along any short cuts, and that the Course, though musical from start to finish, would be neither quick nor easy. d'Indy's motto might well have been that of the Earl of Strafford— " Thorough ". The various courses had been drawn up with the utmost attention to detail and although students would be given certificates stating what grades they had reached, there would be no rewards, awards, or distinctions, since the policy was to produce artists and not mere prize-winners. d'Indy, therefore, made no concession to popular or personal vanity, and those who were not content to work for Arts' sake could stay away. This made for selectivity and might well have resulted in such a small entry of students as to force the institution to close its doors through sheer lack of support. However, it happened the other way, and a vast number of earnest musicians were immediately drawn to it.

No doubt d'Indy had in his mind a venture which would set itself up in open competition with the Conservatoire, but on no occasion did he suggest that this was the case; indeed, when he was asked to take over the orchestral class at the

Conservatoire, he accepted willingly, with the remark that
there was no reason why people should make music against
each other. Actually d'Indy had the whip-hand. In 1892 a
Commission had been formed to draw up a " Projêt d'organisation des études du Conservatoire de musique de Paris ",
d'Indy being a member of the Commission. He himself was
the author of the particular plan, which he referred to as
" L'école répondant aux besoins modernes ". His carefully
thought-out scheme was shelved as being altogether too
revolutionary and nothing further was heard of the proposed
reorganisation. The Schola Cantorum, however, was based
upon this very plan and d'Indy must have smiled quietly to
himself when called by the Conservatoire to put into practice
in his class exactly what had been rejected in 1892. The
proof of the feasibility of the whole thing lies in the fact
of its survival in the face of considerable opposition.

Such a liberal outlook was bound to attract many eminent
musical minds, and among the early professors we find the
names of Guilmant, Albeniz, Roussel (who, having learnt
his craft from Eugéne Gigout (1844-1925) studied form and
orchestration with d'Indy himself during the first two years
of the Schola, remaining a student until 1907, but meanwhile
taking over the counterpoint classes), Pierre de Bréville,
Gabriel Grovlez, Jane Bathori, Blanche Selva, Maurice
Emmanuel, Albéric Magnard, Louis Vierne and Paul le Flem.
Among the students were Erik Satie, Roland Manuel,
Bohuslav Martinu, Déodat de Séverac, Guy de Lioncourt and
Guy Weitz, while others, eminent later in their own countries,
came from all parts of the globe. Branches were formed
in the various provinces of France, and when Guy Ropartz
was appointed Director of the Conservatoire at Nancy, and
later of that at Strasbourg, he reorganised the whole system
of teaching along the lines of the Schola Cantorum.

Into this work d'Indy put all his heart and soul. He
was at last able to direct an institution in the way he considered ideal. The activities included not only frequent public

performances of the standard works, but revivals of the operas of Monteverde and Rameau. A particularly useful venture was the publishing section, which printed not only original modern works but hitherto obscure polyphonic motets, etc. (there had actually been a special course in music-engraving before the reorganisation). d'Indy, however, was no mere musicologist—that is to say, he detested people who poke their noses into things for the sole purpose of gaining notoriety for research with no practical intention. When d'Indy did research work, it was for the purpose of producing and performing some unknown or neglected masterpiece of the past. As regards the original works published by the Schola, the composer paid for the printing and took 90 per cent. royalties on sales. To-day one frowns slightly upon this principle, but printing was not as expensive then as now and, at any rate, the whole system was perfectly reputable.

The Schola Cantorum went through a few crises, but d'Indy was whole-heartedly supported by his first wife (who died in 1906) and with their friends they applied their private fortunes to the venture without in any way assuming absolutely proprietary rights. It remains to mention that a study of the past pupils at the Schola reveals that a vast majority held important appointments in Paris and elsewhere. That some others fell by the wayside stands to reason because of the severity of the training; but none of these ever inveighed against d'Indy himself.

The situation at d'Indy's death requires some explanation. In his will, d'Indy asked that either Louis de Serres or Guy de Lioncourt (who had been associated with him as pupils and later as professors from the very start) should be elected Director. The Advisory Committee recommended the former as Director, the latter as Sub-Director, and Pierre de Bréville as President of the Council. However, there had been a certain element working underground with a view to voting their own candidates into office as soon as d'Indy died. At

the General Meeting this faction set aside d'Indy's right to
will the Schola (which to all intents and purposes was
virtually his own property) to those he selected, and the
voting contradicted the Committee's recommendations. The
step was quite unexpected, and immediately the majority of
the staff resigned, setting up the school elsewhere under a
different name; nearly all the students followed them. The
new venture became known as the Ecole César Franck and
is now in a flourishing condition. The Schola Cantorum has
nothing to do with it. The situation, therefore, is that the
Ecole César Franck represents what was the original Schola
Cantorum, and the two present institutions should not be
confused.

In considering d'Indy as a teacher, it must be realised that
he regarded this work as a mission and not as a means of
earning a livelihood. The two can be, and often are,
combined, of course, but with d'Indy the former was the
guiding influence. What he preached, he practised. He
lived up to his theories in his own works. That he never
wrote an unworthy bar cannot be claimed for him any more
than it can be for the greatest of composers; but he was
always impelled by the highest artistic motives. When the
wealthy American, Mrs. Elissa Hill, commissioned certain
leading composers to write works for her to play on her
saxophone, she probably did not expect a *Choral varié* composed with becoming dignity and classical regard; but this
was typical of d'Indy's seriousness of purpose. Debussy
wrote his *Rapsodie* and was not in the least interested in
it, since he saw a ridiculous side to the performance. d'Indy
possibly also saw this in his mind, but was far too courteous
to let it influence him, and far too great an artist to approach
the commission in a flippant or derisory vein. Consequently, his writing is consistently high-minded.

His *cours* was a long one, lasting anything from seven to ten
years; this he deemed essential since his pupils had to study
every facet of creative Art from its most primitive to its most

sophisticated state. d'Indy aimed at moulding the consummate artist, and he felt that the mere writing of notes and expressing of ideas was not sufficient. The creative artist had to surround himself with an atmosphere of love and well-wishing. d'Indy himself was free from all spite and petty jealousy, as was his idol, Franck, and although he had his own strong views and equally strong prejudices, he never let them come between himself and the personality of the object. He viewed Art broadly and if towards the end of his long life he found that it had swept past him he may be pardoned for giving way to some bitterness of expression. It takes a superhuman to watch much he has striven after and achieved being suddenly pushed aside, and remain tranquil—and d'Indy was not superhuman. Fortunately, he did not try to write like a young man when he was an old one, and his latest works make very little attempt to line themselves up with any of the " -isms " and " -alities " which became fashionable in the 1920's—it is somewhat intriguing to find that d'Indy often referred to the *nineteenth* century as the " silly " one. The singleness of purpose which he pursued in his compositions and in his classes was remarkable.

One can read his monumental *Cours de Composition musicale* with profit and pleasure, finding in it everything one can possibly want to know, and at the same time a good deal to stimulate argument and disagreement. It stops at the beginning of the century. This is unavoidable, of course, but one would give a lot to be able to read d'Indy's analytical views upon Debussy[1] and Ravel. His classes were the object of an enthusiastic discipleship and the four volumes (three " Parts ") constituting the *Cours de Composition musicale* were thus assembled during the actual lectures by Auguste Sérieyx and, after Sérieux' death, by Guy de Lioncourt, under d'Indy's supervision. d'Indy took responsi-

[1] *Pelléas et Mélisande* is analysed in Vol. III, but otherwise there is no mention of Debussy.

bility for the historical sections in Volume Two, and in the Preface to Volume One stated that he agreed with certain theories put forward by Sérieyx and not by himself.

I have mentioned the high-minded point of view from which d'Indy regarded his work. The English student might be slightly repelled by it as he is not accustomed to regard himself as a " microcosm " or think in terms of "Art" unless he is exceptionally reflective. d'Indy's attitude was very different from that of Paul Dukas, who described Brahms as " too much beer and beard ". d'Indy could never have brought himself to speak in this manner, no matter how much he felt like doing so. The principles of the Schola Cantorum were on a very high level and woe betide anyone, professor or student, who did not keep them there. It is interesting to note that when the Chair of Music was initiated at the School of Music, University College, Aberystwyth, Wales, the whole conduct of the department was placed in the hands of a team of musicians from the Schola Cantorum. The outbreak of war prevented this scheme coming to fruition; but there is no doubt that it would have been broadening to have had this infusion of French ideas. It is a pity that an exchange of professors between the two countries seems too complicated to arrange.

d'Indy made it imperative that one and all should study the subject of creative and created music from its earliest conditions. Those who were not prepared so to do did not enter the Schola Cantorum.

It is absolutely necessary to study the *Cours de Composition musicale* in some detail in order to show its vast scope, for, in reality, it is a technical history of music. The absence of an English translation is to be deplored, for the book has been the guiding light of many prominent composers. I am aware that such a consideration may not make very interesting reading, but in a study of d'Indy, mere mention of it is quite inadequate.

The *Cours de Composition musicale* opens with a volume on technique. In the Foreword, d'Indy says:

The intention of the present work is to give the student, who wishes to earn the title of creative artist, a logical knowledge of his art by means of a theoretical study of musical forms, and the application of this theory to the principal works of the master musicians, examined in their chronological order.

The *Cours* in general is divided into three sections:

1. The rhythmic-monodic period, from the third to the thirteenth centuries.
2. The polyphonic period, from the thirteenth to the seventeenth centuries.
3. The metrical period, from the seventeenth century to the present day.

Volume One deals with the first two of these. The material is laid out under the following headings:

Rhythm, the primitive and predominating element of all Art and its special application to music.
Melody, emerging from accent.
Graphic signs, representing rhythm and melody.
Musical forms, limited by these two elements.

This covers the ground of the first section. Then follows:

> Origin and Theory of Harmony,
> Tonality,
> Expression,

followed in turn by a short history of the theory of harmony and its application to simultaneous melodies as practised in the polyphonic period.

The volume concludes with a study of the evolution of

Art, which leads the student to the third main section constituting the rest of the *Cours*.

Volume One, therefore, may be regarded as an elaborate introduction to music as a whole; but d'Indy fills some pages in discussing the nature of Art in general and the constitutional qualities of the artist, which he terms the Introduction.

Each chapter is given a full synopsis and the several headings are dealt with separately in sectional style. Rhythm and melodic accent are treated extremely lucidly and practically. Melody itself is discussed from the point of view of phrase-shape and tonality. d'Indy quotes from Bach, Beethoven (the later Quartets and Symphonies), Weber, Wagner and Franck. These two chapters would appear to cover some ground already tilled in the ordinary basic training, but d'Indy, as I have said, left nothing to chance.

The third chapter, dealing with Notation, is really one for the musical archæologist. d'Indy discusses lute tablature, showing the difference between the German, French and Italian notations. Here one sees his colossal erudition, which far exceeds the essentials of musical composition; the notation of Hucbald (ninth to tenth centuries), Romanus (ninth century) and Herman Contract (eleventh century) —so-called because he suffered from paralysis in his early age (from the Latin *contractus*)—is vastly interesting to read and study, but hardly vital to composition or composers.

In Chapter IV he treats monodic *cantilène* and goes deeply into plainsong notation and symbols. Here he once more becomes practical. In this country, plainsong notation and the Gregorian idiom are not considered as important as in France, and there are many transcriptions of the primitive church music available in terms of modern notation. d'Indy gives the full analysis of Gregorian melodies and shows how they are constructed, at the same time suggesting to the imaginative reader their connection with variation.

A very short chapter follows dealing with the " Chanson populaire ", concentrating upon its shape and modal qualities. Harmony and tonality are discussed, with various diagrams showing the system of tonal relations. The section (in two chapters) ends with quotations from Bach's Fantasia (and Fugue) in G minor, Beethoven's Tenth Quartet and Wagner's *Tristan und Isolde.* Here d'Indy very clearly demonstrates the way to isolate the basic harmonic schemes from the general mass of the non-essential and decorative music. Following this, there is a dissertation upon expression, which d'Indy, in common with Franck, held to be obtained largely by means of modulation. He gives a brief résumé of the history of harmonic research from Rameau to Riemann, showing how composers have successively made new harmonic discoveries.

From this point the *Cours* becomes entirely practical and the two chapters on the Motet and the " Chanson " and Madrigal not only provide an historical survey, but show the technique and underlying principles of such composition. Motets and madrigals are fully analysed, and the method of composition explained. The student here obtains his first glimpse into the mechanism of music, an essential point for him. It was this concentrated attention on such study that roused the opprobrium of d'Indy's enemies and caused them to stigmatise those who followed him as " d'Indyists ", coining the word " d'Indyism " as they had coined " Franckism ". The student is directed to study many works in addition to the sufficiency of musical quotations. d'Indy's own students had the benefit of the earlier *Anthologie.*[1]

The point that may strike the English reader here is the complete absence of any consideration of our own polyphonic school other than the mention of a few names, included, one feels, rather grudgingly. The *Cours* was given before the period of enlightenment, when the Elizabethans were sung unobtrusively in cathedrals on Fridays ("unaccompanied days "), and Dr. E. H. Fellowes had not yet

[1] See page 14.

produced his wonderful editions showing up the many faults of the earlier versions and revealing the many beauties. Our polyphonic composers had not reached the Continent and Continental musicians contented themselves with Palestrina. England was still regarded as the land without music. That d'Indy would have waxed enthusiastic over our composers is undoubted, and it is lamentable that in spite of the efforts of such organisations as the British Council to disseminate our culture abroad, French musicians concerned with polyphonic music are still in comparative unawareness of what we can show.[1]

The chapter on the evolution of music is sufficiently concise to form a connecting episode or bridge passage to the second part. d'Indy does not himself provide any " exercises ", but in an Appendix gives directions to the reader which should be carried out under the supervision of his teacher.[2] He lays final emphasis upon the value of the Chorale-Prelude as exemplified by Bach as a means of acquiring facility in melodic development and variation.

It may be conceded that the greater part of this first volume is rather dry, and it is difficult to see how it could be otherwise; but it is in no way a conventional *textbook*, and the reader gets the clear impression that he is reading a book about music and not a musical grammar.

Volume Two is at once most comprehensive and debatable. In Volume One d'Indy gave all the evidence of his powerful scholarship and erudition. In Volume Two the scholarship is no less marked, but it is of a different nature. Volume One was concerned with matters which raise no argument. Volume Two is sufficiently polemical to prove its vitality.

---

[1] Would it not be better to spend some of the money laid out upon sending pianists all over Europe to play Chopin and Rachmaninoff (which the foreign pianists play just as well) in propagating the interest in our polyphonic music by means of lectures illustrated with gramophone records? The British Council complains that it has insufficent money for such lectures, but is not this missionary work one primary reason for its existence?

[2] Who will, of course, have read the book himself.

d'Indy did not come out with any statement which may be described as " outrageous ", but he frequently put forward theories which are not always convincing at first glance, and in some cases at neither second nor third. One cannot find fault with this, and it is refreshing to read what is virtually a textbook (in spite of its attractive format) whose dogmatism is sufficiently provoking to cause disagreement; d'Indy's accuracy, however, cannot be questioned.

This enormous Volume Two, Part One, deals with Fugue, Suite, Sonata, and Variation. It is introduced in a chapter which fully explains the origin of what d'Indy generalises as " symphonic music ", classifies the several genres and shows the balance between musical composition and architectural construction, d'Indy quoting at some length from Ruskin's *Seven Lamps of Architecture.*

The first section deals with Fugue and Canon, the examples being drawn from the more unfamiliar works. d'Indy draws a clear distinction between the " classroom fugue " and that conceived by the composer, including in the Appendix a comprehensive plan of the layout of the former.

d'Indy treats Canon and Ricercare from the strictly academic point of view, drawing his examples mainly from Bach—both *The Art of Fugue* and *A Musical Offering* are brought into use. This section does not show a very clear dividing line between the basic training and composition, and this is apparent also in the opening paragraphs on Fugue which give definitions and explanations that the student may well be expected to know already. However, a résumé of this nature is not out of place. In order to show the difference between classroom and composer's Fugue, d'Indy analyses the *Organ Fugue in C,* whose subject is:

Ex.1

which fully illustrates Bach's approach to what, later,

became quite wrongly recognised as a technical exercise (in the days of Cherubini (1760-1842) Fugue was considered nothing more than a kind of mental and theoretical musical drill, with no thought of the musical possibilities of the texture). d'Indy's complete analysis of this particular Fugue is masterly in the way it avoids stating its vagaries from textbook principles. He does not make it clear at what point or for what reason the classroom Fugue came into actual existence or why Bach's " textbooks " mentioned above were not adopted in the first place. The laws of tonal relationship are explained very lucidly by means of diagrams.

The general principle underlying this section explores each constituent part of the Fugue in turn.

Having covered the constructional and architectural ground, d'Indy follows with one of his famous historical sections, in which the reader is taken through the progress of Fugue from the primitive Italian, Spanish, English, German and French composers. Here he pays tribute to Tallis and Byrd, the former in a three-line biographical paragraph, the latter by quoting *Non nobis, Domine*. If only he had known our other composers and, particularly, the Motet in 40 parts by Tallis, the value of the book would have been enhanced. The German, Netherlandic and Danish music is placed in one category and, contrary to what might have been expected, he devotes only a page and a half to the primitive French school.

This is followed by a study of the " Période de Floraison", which means "J. S. Bach ". Taking the organ fugues as his models, he draws attention to certain salient features, such as the canonic climaxes in the *Fantasia (and Fugue) in G minor*. Both *The Art of Fugue* and *A Musical Offering* are analysed in part, but the student is referred to the *Forty-Eight* instead of being spoon-fed with them.

The post-Bach composers are considered in a separate section which he calls the " Modern Period ". This includes a résumé of the *Grosse Fuge* of Beethoven and carries the study rather quickly as far as Franck (whose *Prélude, Choral et Fugue* comes in for thematic explanation), and Saint-Saëns.

Much is left to the student to ferret out for himself. Having put him upon the road to discovery, d'Indy rightly feels that further analysis should be a matter of personal enterprise.

From Fugue we proceed to Suite. This explanation is unique in its completeness and interest. It puts the mathematical side of form completely in the shade and shows how the whole thing became an evolutionary process. The Suite is first discussed as a whole, each movement in turn being then subjected to minute examination. He shows how the early Italian *Sonata* of Scarlatti was formed upon some dance rhythm and style, and leads the reader to that moment when the multi-movement *Suite* merged into the multi-movement *Sonata*. The reader will find that not only are Rameau and Bach closely studied, but many unknown Italians also, and he who regards this genre as simply a stringing together of certain short and undeveloped monothematic pieces, will find that there is more than meets the eye. The historical survey again testifies to d'Indy's scholarship, but it goes no further than J. S. Bach, save to mention Alexis de Castillon a favourite pupil of César Franck, whose two *Suites for Piano* are indicated as examples of later-day Dance Suites imagined upon the lines of the earlier composers. There was no reason at the time the *Cours* was compiled why discussion should go further than Bach; only since the beginning of the century have composers returned to the classical Suite design with any increasing frequency, and it rather looks as if d'Indy mentioned de Castillon simply because they were personal friends and members of the " Franck Family ".[1]

The Sonata is taken through its pre-Beethoven state, each

[1] If the reader will turn to page 51, he will find an interesting return to the old-style Suite design on the part of d'Indy himself.

movement being treated separately as in the case of the Suite.
The usual definitions open the chapter and the progress of
the genre is shown very graphically through the works of
C. P. E. Bach, Haydn and Mozart. d'Indy thus traces its
course to its ultimate state of a " cycle of movements ".
Once more the historical section is of the utmost value.
Having disposed of the immediate pre-Beethoven principle
of ternary form, he returns to the primitive state in the
Sonatas of J. S. Bach, this leading immediately to the bi-
thematicism as established by C. P. E. Bach (whose
important Sonatas are treated in detailed manner with
copious illustration) and Haydn. d'Indy draws attention to
certain anticipations which find their fruition in Beethoven,
notably the rhythm of the middle section of Haydn's Sonata
in E flat, which he feels to have given Beethoven the idea
for the well-known four-quaver figure in the *Appasionata*:

One is not altogether convinced here since this particular
rhythm is by no means uncommon in the history of music.

Mozart is treated rather briefly. d'Indy regarded him as
" musiquette ", a not unusual attitude at the time when
Mozartean enlightenment was not what it is now. Haydn
he regarded as greater than Mozart, and the analyses of
Haydn's Sonatas are well-balanced.

During the course of his researches into pre-Beethoven Sonata, d'Indy discovered a set of such works by Friedrich Wilhelm Rust (1739-1796). These appeared so far in advance of the technique of their period that d'Indy felt himself justified in regarding their composer as the immediate precursor of Beethoven, and devoted ten pages to him. It became known in some way or other that these works had been edited and modernised by Rust's grandson, Wilhelm (1822-1892). This d'Indy duly noted in a footnote, but his opponents took up the cudgel and prepared to beat him. Saint-Saëns, redoubtably set against all forms of Franckism and d'Indyism, made great play with the credulity of d'Indy in his little book, *Les Idées de M. Vincent d'Indy*, and attempted to belittle his foe in the eyes of the musical world. What Saint-Saëns did not know, however, was that d'Indy copied the original Rust MSS. as deposited in the Conservatoire in Berlin. Saint-Saëns could produce no documentary evidence whatsoever and had written entirely on hearsay. He retracted in a letter to d'Indy,[1] who, meanwhile, had edited the Sonatas in question and had sent them for publication to Rouart-Lerolle—this happened in 1919; the reader will find further discussion of the Saint-Saëns-d'Indy " affaire " on page 41 of this book.

The discovery of these Sonatas was an event of considerable importance, for they narrow the gap between Haydn and Beethoven and show a smoother evolutionary process in the Sonata than that indicated directly from the one composer to the other. d'Indy did not maintain that Rust's Sonatas were great works, but he certainly showed their importance, and it is regrettable that historians have swallowed the story of the imposture without questioning. There are many more points of contact between Rust and Beethoven than between the latter and Haydn.

d'Indy's section on Beethoven's Piano Sonatas is worthy of

[1] See *La Revue Musicale*, February 1947, where Léon Vallas prints unpublished letters of both composers on this subject.

separate publication. He does not approach them from the Tovey angle of " from the first note to the last ", but uses the works to examine the whole question of the Sonata principle in 142 pages of fully illustrated explanation, indicating points of contact with Beethoven's predecessors. Although the main matter of the Sonata in general is concerned with those written for the piano, the section closes with an analysis of those for the violin and the 'cello. The entire question of tonal relationship and formal balance is discussed, and d'Indy, using the " Hammerklavier " Sonata as his example, shows the growth of the initial idea to its fullest expansion. This is the real art of teaching composition as far as it can be taught. He takes the student through each type of movement separately, pointing out exactly how the themes are balanced and opposed to each other. Every player should study these pages, for d'Indy is always careful to emphasise the musical achievements of the processes. A great deal is assumed on the part of the student, and he has to read d'Indy as a supplement to his basic formal training. It is not a question of saying that " this is this " and " that is that ", a method which is extremely valuable and which Tovey achieved in his own masterly and individual manner. Tovey's is aimed more at the neophyte, and no one could deal with this type of student better than he.

The panorama from Beethoven to the modern period includes the style known as *cyclique* which has probably caused more argument and disagreement than most other facets of music. Franck, noticing that certain Beethoven works were connected up by means of permutations or fragments of themes, came to the conclusion that this process was a most logical one, and was capable of giving a multi-movement work entire cohesion. His greatest fulfilment of this ideal can be found in the *Prélude, Aria et Final*, whose material finds its origin in various short strands which, on their first appearance, are seemingly contained within the texture and are in no way thematically significant at the time. In other places there is distinct relationship between one theme and another, and also definite quotation. Franck, however, never taught this to his pupils. They found it out for themselves while studying his works. The cyclical idea is somewhat similar to the germinal principle practised by Sibelius (1865), but the former is more concerned with actual quotation than is the latter.

There is divergence of opinion as to the actual meaning of the term *cyclique*. Some hold that it refers to the cycle of keys through which the music passes, with a tonic fulcrum; others, that it is merely a cycle of movements—as has been stated, d'Indy himself so described a certain evolutionary point in the Sonata. It seems obvious, however, to apply the style to those works which either find their thematic content in permutations of earlier material, or refer to it by quotation in part or in whole from movement to movement. d'Indy investigated the whole matter and made certain deductions from pre-Beethoven works and from those of Beethoven. In many cases the theory is fully justified.

There is no doubt about examples like these:

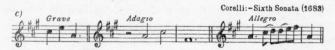

while the following quotations from Beethoven should answer the doubters:

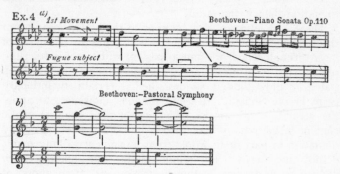

In the latter case the arpeggio figure provides some material for the commentator.

The connection by quotation in Beethoven's Fifth Symphony and *Sonata Pathétique* does not provide actual authority, since Beethoven did not adopt it as a habit; the last movement of the Ninth is exceptional, of course, in view of the intention of the closing choral variations, to Schiller's text.

d'Indy did not impose this process upon his pupils any more than did Franck. Franck used it in his early Trio in B flat, Op. 2, and in this particular work altered the form by putting the second subject before the first in the recapitulation, thus placing the two subjects in exactly their opposite positions. Franck and Liszt were the first to adopt the cyclical idea in general practice. Brahms touched it, notably in the Piano Sonata in C; but d'Indy, from the moment he grasped its resultant cohesion, never departed from it.

The popular view of d'Indy's Schola Cantorum teaching

was that he compelled everybody to conform with his own idea. The fallacy of this lies in the distinguished pupils who studied there, none of whom would have been willing to renounce their independence or individuality. What he did impose was a rigid discipline in the basic training, and an insistence upon seriousness of purpose. It is a striking tribute to his genius and powers as a teacher that he split musicians into two factions—cyclique and anti-cyclique—a situation which, if it did not lead to violence of action, certainly led to violence of argument and to enthusiastic partisanship. Unfortunately for themselves, certain composers whose works were written in strict accord with the " system " joined the " anti-cyclique " faction.

The volume ends with a masterly and complete section on the Variation in all its styles. One may possibly ask why it appears at this point instead of after the Suite, seeing that it is so closely knit with the middle or development section of the Sonata. d'Indy goes as far as his own " Istar " Variations and Dukas' monumental set upon a theme by Rameau.

Part Two carries the discussion of form and style into the realms of Concerto, Symphony, " Accompanied " Chamber Music, String Quartet, Concert (or Symphonic) Overture, Symphonic Poem and " Fantaisie ". He shows quite clearly how these genres differ from the actual formal processes and manner of the Sonata, which he considers something quite separate and distinct. In this theory he emphasises its isolation. His classicism is indicated in his refusal to acknowledge a Symphony with a programmatic basis as anything but an enlarged Symphonic Poem, an attitude with which many will not agree. He requires from its genre something deeper than mere entertainment music. His admiration of Schumann does not blind him to the literal transposition of some of the recapitulation sections in the Symphonies, and a work of the nature of Grieg's Piano Concerto is relegated to the ranks of a Symphonic Poem without any programme.

He requires these established formalistic works to be absolutely abstract.

All this follows a unique Introduction dealing with orchestration. After discussing the potentialities of each instrument, he gives lists of suitable and unsuitable combinations. This I have been unable to find in any other standard book on the subject, most of which content themselves with skimming over the surface in a general manner, leaving it to the instinct of the reader to judge for himself. d'Indy's musical bible in his youth had been Berlioz' *Instrumentation*, which he studied in complete detail and which aroused an early enthusiasm for Gluck and Meyerbeer (incredible though the inclusion of the latter may seem). d'Indy on the orchestra, therefore, may be regarded as supplemental to Berlioz on the same subject.

A very important discussion in this part is devoted to "Accompanied" Chamber Music and to the String Quartet which finds no parallel anywhere that I can find, save in *Chamber Music*, by Thomas F. Dunhill,[1] a treatise devoted more to the mechanics of writing the music than to a consideration of structural methods. d'Indy once more places the genres in line with the Sonata and shows the similarity and dissimilarity of the two approaches. The same process is gone through regarding the Concerto and Symphonic Poem, and the reader is left in no doubt on the matter.

Volume Three deals with dramatic music.

d'Indy puts forward a very personal point of view on the subject with which the majority of readers will disagree; but this does not imply that either d'Indy or the reader is necessarily wrong. d'Indy deals with dramatic music, oratorio and cantata, incidental music and, surprisingly, song. In a footnote, M. Guy de Lioncourt explains that this is put first in the *Cours* as now run at the Ecole César Franck. The importance of this volume lies not in the method of teaching the student " how to write an opera, etc." (which

[1] Macmillan.

is absurd), but in the interesting way in which the several genres are discussed historically and technically, although the book is the least technical of the three volumes. It is also extremely interesting for readers imbued with the English traditional manner of looking at things, to see certain much-beloved works relegated rather to the background, and their importance rated considerably below what we feel it to be.[1] Again, this was d'Indy's point of view and any author who satisfies everybody by writing what he knows his readers want to read is indeed a dull dog, and the reader who wants what he reads to coincide with his own views is even duller. It is certainly true to say that the reader will be considerably astonished as he peruses the book, but on mature reflection, he may agree, realising that d'Indy's attitude had never occurred to him.

Although d'Indy takes the reader through the " story " of many an opera, he does so by combining the musical matter with the episodes he describes. He divides the various periods of opera into three, " Preparation ", " Floraison "[2] and " Result ".

Broadly speaking, he divides the whole history of opera into three epochs, the Italian (from Monteverde to Scarlatti), the French (Lully to Méhul and to Debussy) and the German (Weber to Wagner). As regards the third epoch, M. de Lioncourt adds an informative tailpiece to each culture which brings the story almost to the actual present day. It is, alas, impossible here to give a detailed analysis of this valuable and debatable volume which is a history of opera in its truest sense. It will have to suffice to draw attention to certain salient features. d'Indy does not mince his words: " He made [sic] 12 operas, lacking in personality, and not concealing any of the faults of the ' verist ' school. However,

---

[1] Particularly *The Messiah*.

[2] I use this French term advisedly as it is more expressive than its English counterpart.

his style is perhaps less abominably commonplace than that
of Leoncavallo." With which opinion of Puccini, the
reader must content himself, but the temptation to quote
further is difficult to resist.

d'Indy lays great stress upon the tonal relationships which
he shows to play a great part in the thought of all operatic
composers. He quotes facts which relate tonalities to
characters and episodes, particularly in Wagner, and thus
puts forward a completely individual aspect of operatic construction. The reader realises that it is as necessary to attend
a *Cours* in Opera as it is in Sonata or Symphony. It is
generally conceded in this country, apparently, that one
requires very little, if any, special operatic or dramatic
training to compose an opera;[1] but composers do not have
any great encouragement offered them, and this deficiency
has resulted in a general qualification of opera " not being
for us ". d'Indy's opinions are valuable and worth debating.
It is when we get to Oratorio and Cantata that we begin to
feel really surprised. d'Indy appears to have been slightly
puzzled by the English meaning of the word " anthem ",
for in a paragraph devoted to Purcell, he categorises certain
anthems as cantatas, placing them next to the less ambitious
works of the kind by J. S. Bach. He does, however, see
the influence of Purcell in Handel, particularly in the
oratorio *Esther*. He divides oratorio into two qualities, the
Lyrical and Epic, the former quality ending with Haydn,
whose *The Creation* is sympathetically dealt with. The
latter commences with Beethoven and concludes with
Glazounov, including Wagner and Elgar (who is given a
" sympathetic notice " in a few lines, but no analysis).

Our first real shock is to find Wagner's *The Ring* included
en masse as an Epic Oratorio. It is worth quoting d'Indy's
explanation of this:

Das Ring der Nibelungen, in spite of its stage repre-

[1] It is undoubtedly the reason why the majority of English operas
are sterile.

sentation, may be considered as the first musical epic poem. It admirably fulfils all the requirements, and shows the weaknesses. Wagner wished to establish a German type of epic poem; he carried to it his genius and his exaggerations. In comparison with *Tristan*, *Die Meistersinger*, and *Parsifal*, it is not the stage which is pre-eminent in *Das Ring*.

This is as may be and it is a point of view which I have found nowhere else. It seems to be contained in the opinion that there is not enough stage action and that the music is too continuously concerned with epic poetry. This section should be read with an open mind. There is nothing outrageous about it if one concedes the point that individuals may hold their own theories and opinions, and that when these are held by an artist of the calibre and importance of Vincent d'Indy, they are entitled to our regard and consideration.

Incidental music, or *musique de scène*, covers ballet (i.e. *air de ballet*, pantomime, or music accompanying gesture) and incidental music itself which, had d'Indy been alive to-day, would have included that for films and radio. Ballet goes no further than Léo Delibes (1836-1891) and Edouard Lalo (1823-1892). d'Indy is particularly informative on the opera-ballets of Lully and Rameau; would that he could have written upon the revival of this manner as exemplified by his pupil, Albert Roussel, in *Padmâvati*.

Pantomime represents the " musical expression of sentiments and passion ". The division between it and ballet is not very clear unless one realises that by the latter d'Indy means the actual ballet or dancing music. His view on the former can be seen by his choice of examples, which include the scene of " Love being sent to sleep by Jealousy " from Rameau's *Dardanus*, the sung ballet of birds in Gluck's *Armide*, the " Chasse Royale " in Berlioz' *Les Troyens*, and the " Washing of the Feet " in *Parsifal*. d'Indy makes no attempt to discuss dancers or actual dancing and the section is the shortest in the whole *Cours*. Similarly terse is that on incidental music and both sections appear to have been included in order to make the *Cours* complete; but the considerations of Beethoven's music for *Egmont*, Mendelssohn's for *A Midsummer Night's Dream*, and Ernest Chausson's (1885-1899) score for Bouchon's *mystère* " Sainte Cécile ", music and play both being completely unknown in this country, are complete and sympathetic.

Song is divided into *chanson populaire*, *lied musical* (Beethoven, Schubert, etc.)—in this section he includes Grieg—*lied dramatique* (from de Castillon to Debussy), the whole thing being brought up-to-date by M. de Lioncourt in a categorised chronicle. The reader is shown the difference between the *Lied per se* and what is known as the *Lied form*, or ordinary ternary ABA design, used extensively in the book on the Sonata. d'Indy, frankly, might have been a little more technical here, but doubtless he considered that the ground had been covered by the first volume in the chapter on melody. Certain aspects of melodic construction are treated in an Appendix by Guy de Lioncourt.

This particular volume is most stimulating because of the points of obvious disagreement made possible by d'Indy's own particular points of view. The reader must remember that it was written at the beginning of the century and try and curb his disappointment when each actual d'Indy chapter ends just at the time when his interest has been fully aroused. He may like to compare this volume with an earlier one on the same subject by Antonin Reicha (1770-1836), *Art du compositeur dramatique, ou cours complet de composition vocale*, which may be picked up now and again in second-hand bookshops and bookstalls. Reicha attempted to teach students " how to write an opera "; d'Indy showed how others have written them and has worked upon the principle of emulation and not that of pure dogmatic technical pedagogy. Reicha, however, has some sound advice to give upon dramatic points, which still concern opera composers.

There is small wonder that d'Indy's polemical and altogether outstanding book played straight into the hands of his opponents, who seized upon his outspoken theories and tried to destroy them; but it still stands supreme and unique, and the reputation of its author has gained in stature accordingly. The enmity and petty spite continued over a number of years, and by degrees the smaller Hanslicks and Chorleys retired, defeated and discomfited. Only one doughty critic refused to realise that the *Cours* had won the day, and he, to the last, kept up a continual stream of vitriolic abuse.

The opposition to d'Indy and his teaching methods came to a head in 1919, when Camille Saint-Saëns published his afore-mentioned[1] *Les Idées de M. Vincent d'Indy*, which was a critical review of the book. It may be wondered why Saint-Saëns waited until 1919 seeing that Volume One of the *Cours* was published in 1903 and the second in 1909. During the First Great War d'Indy and Saint-Saëns found themselves on opposite sides over the Wagner question— should Wagner be played in France during the War or should he not; should, indeed, any German music be played? d'Indy, with Ravel and others, could see no reason why he should not (he would have thought differently in the Second World War), Saint-Saëns and a few others considered that he had exercised sufficient influence on French music and in view of Hans Sachs' exhortation at the end of *Die Meistersinger*, felt that he should be barred. The whole thing was rather trivial up to a point, and it served to estrange the two composers even further. Saint-Saëns, nearing the end of his life, found the iron had entered into his soul and determined to try and settle the Franck-d'Indy question once and for all.

Here a curious situation arose which in all probability could happen nowhere but in France. Saint-Saëns sent d'Indy a set of proofs of the book which was to pulverise

[1] Page 31.

4

him, with a polite note, explaining that had he, like d'Indy, been surrounded with pupils, he would have adopted other methods of expressing his disapproval and disagreement with d'Indy's work. Saint-Saëns stated that he realised the importance of d'Indy's work, and ended the letter with expressions of high esteem. d'Indy, being exceedingly busy, postponed his answer for some while. It was couched in the most courteous terms and contained no rancour—in fact, d'Indy said that he was extremely honoured that Saint-Saëns should have taken the trouble to read his book. Only one detail roused his ire, and that was a section dealing quite gratuitously with Franck, whom Saint-Saëns insulted and deprecated in a manner which showed that his early anti- pathy and hostility had not in any way diminished. In any other country this belated and sarcastic criticism would have resulted in expressions of personal animosity. d'Indy, how- ever, in his detailed reply undertook not to show the matter to the Press, as he considered it to be a question between himself and Saint-Saëns, and not one for all the journalists to take sides over. Saint-Saëns, in his reply, agreed. The whole matter was conducted with model politeness and restraint, and actually resulted in a resumption of the early friendship between the two composers. Saint-Saëns was defeated all along the line simply because he overstated his case.

From among the many points which Saint-Saëns queried in his book (d'Indy did not answer them all), we may select denials of d'Indy's theory that music had its origin in sacred music and that expression should be put into music of the sixteenth century. In the latter case Saint-Saëns bore out his argument by stating that when a young man he had heard the choir of the Sistine Chapel singing this music at a perfectly level dynamic. Over the whole question d'Indy asked Saint- Saëns if he had never vibrated at the spiritual passion of this music which contained its own expression. He said outright that Saint-Saëns had not the slightest idea of what he was talking about and could not know the music, this having its possibly desired effect in making Saint-Saëns air his knowledge. Another point for anger was a " rall " which d'Indy had inserted in a Bach piece, Saint-Saëns stating that as Bach had not inserted it, it should not appear. d'Indy replied that the freedom of Gregorian lyricism called for it and that Bach, after all, wrote lyrical melody of a similar freedom. The " affaire Rust " called for a retraction by Saint-Saëns, as has been stated.

However, the crowning iniquity was this gratuitous insult hurled at Franck, twenty-eight years after his death, aimed, of course, at d'Indy's adoration of Franck as a man and a musician. Saint-Saëns described Franck's teaching as consisting for the most part of " compliments and encouragements which, coming from one so exalted, enchanted the pupils and made enthusiastic proselytes and disciples ". d'Indy ignored this, for how could Saint-Saëns know— indeed, his statement was borne out only by the case of Duparc (1848-1933), who consulted Saint-Saëns over the orchestration of his Symphonic Poem Lénore, and in spite of Saint-Saëns' work, continued to call himself Franck's pupil. The fact was that Franck did not consider himself a master of orchestration and Vincent d'Indy at the time had not advanced sufficiently to enable him to take students on for this subject. Saint-Saëns considered Franck more a musician than an artist and denied him any poetic qualities. Saint-Saëns detested the whole Franckian concept of music, particularly as exemplified in the Prélude, Choral et Fugue, which he described as a piece " ungracious and uncomfortable to play, where the Choral is not a choral and the Fugue is not a fugue ". d'Indy hotly refuted this in turn, saying that he considered the fugue to be " perfectly regular and infinitely more musical than the learned lucubrations [sic] of Cherubini ". Saint-Saëns' objection to a certain change of tonality was met by a similar objection to one of his own. Saint-Saëns also accused d'Indy of being influenced by

Riemann and other "Westphalian" theorists, to which d'Indy replied that he had merely chronicled these theories and had in fact written some strong letters to Combarieu, a French musicologist and pupil of Spitta, in which he poured ridicule on the German theories and theorists. In the correspondence each composer repeatedly assured the other of the high esteem in which he held his opponent, and the whole thing was carried on in the most dignified manner by d'Indy, who must have hurt Saint-Saëns considerably by his refusal to be drawn to anger by every remark save one. Saint-Saëns closed the discussion by saying that it was not his fault that Franck's music "bored him"; but that hardly justified the venomous onslaught which he made upon a dead man. He may have been only too glad that d'Indy expressed his intention of keeping the matter private. In the circumstances, d'Indy would have had every right to answer the criticisms in public. Saint-Saëns was then seventy-five years old and thoroughly disillusioned and this may well have suggested the feasibility of not bringing the old man into possible ridicule, for Saint-Saëns' influence had already faded away.[1]

I have dealt with this *Cours de Composition musicale* at this length because it is one of the most important books in existence. The entire *Cours* takes a very long time to complete, and its value *in toto* cannot be over-estimated. If all instrumentalists had to go through it, they would have a clearer insight into things than seems to be usually the case; it does not teach anyone how to compose—those who profess

[1] In point of fact, Saint-Saëns and Franck must be the most astonished of spirits when they see the complete reversal of their respective positions. Saint-Saëns who, in his lifetime, ranked among the most widely performed and fêted of representative French composers, now counts for absolutely nothing, while Franck, the despised and rejected of composers outside the circle of a few faithful admirers, has a permanent and frequent place in the repertoire. Franck must have smiled contentedly when his *Variations Symphoniques* were played and danced at Covent Garden on a Gala Night, the distinguished audience including the King of England and the President of the French Republic.

to do this by rote are attempting an impossibility. It does, however, teach how composers have composed, and this knowledge is essential to all musicians and music-lovers.

As a writer on music, d'Indy left a polemical book on Beethoven and a short study of Wagner. The latter does not go very far, as d'Indy died before completing it, but the former propagates some theories which do not seem to have occurred to the usual commentators. He was an indefatigable writer to the musical Press. Unfortunately, his articles are scattered over a wide range of journals and are not available in book form. They express his own views in no uncertain manner, for he was quite unable to resist the temptation to answer all theories which did not agree with his. The time is ripe for their publication although they refer mostly to contemporary matters which have been solved in course of time. However, the opinions of such a distinguished man cannot but be of the greatest interest and importance, even though the subjects have long ago been settled or faded into the background.

Such of the articles as one has come across reveal great breadth of mind and sympathy with æthetics directly in opposition to his own. While Saint-Saëns gave up his usual summer holiday in order to cry-down Debussy's *Pelléas et Mélisande* before he had heard a note of it,[1] d'Indy had recognised its latent possibilities as a genuine art expression, although disagreeing with the technique and approach to the subject. This he demonstrated in an article written the day before the actual production (in Paris the dress rehearsal is regarded as a kind of " Press show "). Privately, he did not think that it would live because of its absence of form, but he appreciated its sincerity and genuine attempt to say something original and thus put forward a new point of view and conception of the lyric stage. This is objectivity at its highest point. It may be mentioned in passing that no matter how unkindly Debussy may have spoken of other

[1] *De Rameau à Ravel,*—Pierre Lalo (Albin Michel)

French composers, he never wrote of Franck, Chausson, d'Indy or Dukas other than with the highest respect and admiration. The very worst he could say of d'Indy's great opera L'Etranger[1] was that it contained " too much music ".

d'Indy himself had no great opinion of criticism, and it may be fitting to conclude this section by quoting from an article which appeared in La Révue d'art dramatique, 5 February 1899:

> I consider that criticism is useless, I would even say that it is harmful. . . . Criticism generally means the opinion some man or other holds about another person's work. How can this opinion help forward the growth of Art? It is interesting to know the ideas, even the erroneous ideas, of geniuses and men of great talent, such as Goethe, Schumann, Wagner, Saint-Beuve, and Micheles when they wish to indulge in criticism; but it is of no interest at all to know whether Mr. So-and-So likes, or does not like, such-and-such dramatic or musical work.

The only point upon which one might argue with this opinion is whether criticism actually does any harm in the long run, especially when written by the Mr. So-and-Sos whose name is Legion.

---

[1] See page 90 et seq.

CHAPTER THREE

The Composer

I. GENERAL SURVEY

D'INDY touched almost every genre and, like the majority of eclectic composers, was more successful in some than in others. His compositions start in the year 1869 and include a song, an unfinished opera, a piano sonata and a symphony, all of which were destroyed. The first presentable work was spread over the period 1878-1888 and consisted of a Piano Quartet in A which is suspected of containing the elements of the early quartet he showed to Franck, with such devastating results—" You know nothing at all ".[1] During this period, however, he wrote what many consider to be his first really representative work, the three symphonic overtures known collectively as *Wallenstein*. It is difficult to follow the course of the Quartet since the particular ten years between conception and fruition were remarkably prolific, and it would appear that d'Indy worked at it sporadically and with little enthusiasm.

Wallenstein has often been played here. Not so the enormous *Le Chant de la Cloche* (1879-1883), a dramatic legend, after Schiller, for soloists, double choir and orchestra. This work established d'Indy's reputation as a composer and placed him in the forefront of European music. It is one of those works which indicate a historical peak as well as being an oasis in a desert of otherwise rather indifferent music. It was, however, in 1886 that he finally placed himself among

[1] *César Franck*, d'Indy (The Bodley Head).

composers of the highest rank with the *Symphonie sur un chant montagnard français* for orchestra and piano (note this description, as it is important).

In 1881 he had commenced the composition of his first music drama, *Fervaal*, which was not completed until 1895. d'Indy, therefore, was always in the position of working at several compositions at the same time. The *Symphonie Cévenole*, to give the above work its short title, opened a new vista on the concertante principle, and it aroused no hostility worth considering. *Fervaal*, however, was another story and its symphonic propensities immediately raised a storm of indignation among those who saw in it a direct attempt to impinge Wagnerism on French Art. We shall see how and why this idea prevailed, and how very slender were the foundations for the charge.

The next important works were the *Istar Variations* (1896), the Second String Quartet (1897) and the second music-drama, *L'Etranger* (1898-1901). At this point d'Indy's music appeared regularly in concert programmes, and his reputation began to spread all over Europe, with the exception of this country which, still under the influence of Brahms, remained oblivious to the solid figure placing French music upon a universal basis. From this moment d'Indy composed all those works which are perfectly acceptable to-day—only those of the earlier period mentioned above are so. d'Indy confirmed his Schola Cantorum lectures by his own musical example. Consequently, we have to record at least three works which irrefutably carry out his theories. These works are the Second Symphony in B flat (1902-1903), *Jour d'Eté à la Montagne* (1905) described as " *trois pièces pour orchestre* " but is virtually a third Symphony, and the Piano Sonata in E (1907). These three works alone are sufficient to establish the high claims that his admirers put forward for him.

He seems to have worked quicker from this moment and to have been content with one work at a time, with the exception of the sacred drama *La Légende de Saint-Christophe*, which occupied him from 1908-1918. His style began to change after the completion of this work. He became increasingly drawn to the early Suite and Sonata manner. An amazingly fresh *Concert* for flute, 'cello, piano and strings (1926) indicated that he was fully capable of writing in a neo-classical style if he wished, although not prepared to go as far as to acknowledge the fashionable " -isms " and " -alities " or the iconoclastic practices of certain of Les Six.

Now and again one comes across the old Adam which could never entirely desert him, and a work like the *Thème varié, Fugue et Chanson* for piano (1925) is Franckist in all its elements—and none the worse for that. Certain large works came from his pen—the *Poème des Rivages* (1919-1920) and the *Diptyque Méditerranéen* (1925-1926), both for orchestra, showed that his fine brain was not in any way tiring or deteriorating with increasing age, and both works have a freshness about them which many a younger composer could indeed envy. In 1922-1923 he essayed a " comédie-musicale ", *Le Rêve de Cinyras*, which astonished those who had come to expect only austerity and classic formality from him. Consequently, it was some while before a producer would undertake it, since such a work from such a composer could hardly be expected to be a box office certainty or attraction. When eventually it was produced, it caused a mild sensation.

His Sonata for 'cello and piano (1924-1925), his Suite for flute, violin, viola, 'cello and harp (1927) and Sextet for two violins, two violas, and two 'cellos (1928) show a surprisingly youthful simplicity without being in any way naïve. In 1928-1929 he composed a third String Quartet and, when he died, sketches were found for a fourth. This strictly early-classical style was not unexpected from a man of his age. Others had found their ultimate happiness in small forms, but few have been so convincingly successful, for

ideas came to d'Indy with no slackening of impulse. Turning
to slender textures in late years is the usual course of events.
Beethoven found solace in the Quartet, Debussy in the
little classically-designed Sonatas composed by the *musicien
français* and it is by no means certain that he fully convinced
his admirers that the style really suited him or was genuinely
and subconsciously inspired. The gap between Debussy's
generally recognised music and this late classicism was very
wide; in the case of d'Indy the only differentiation was
between the Franckian range of harmony and the classical
simplicity. It is not without significance that the Scherzo
from the Sextet was encored at its first performance on 26
January 1929. It would appear that Parisian audiences
found no wide space between the neo-classicism of Les Six
and everything that they were treated to at that period, and
the pure classicism of d'Indy. He was right to compose this
music in his own natural style rather than make an attempt
to bring himself " up-to-date ".

It is interesting to note that it is these small works which
keep him in the line of the growth of music until his death,
and not a late large-scale one like the Sinfonia Brevis (*De
Bello Gallico*) composed in 1917-1918, which says very little
other than what he said before and whose attempts at
realistic contrast between French and German are rather
unsuccessful. d'Indy was always much concerned in his
music with the struggle between Good and Evil. The
Symphony in B flat finds its foundation upon this philosophy.
He was more successful in the music dramas by reason of the
text—an obvious statement, of course. When it came to
actual representation of concrete fact in symphonic music,
he failed because the matter was too materialistic. Others
have similarly failed—Elgar's Demons in *The Dream of
Gerontius*, if not particularly demoniacal, are altogether
unconvincing when they become Germans in *The Fourth of
August*, an otherwise impressive and deeply-felt little work, as
are the two other parts which constitute *The Spirit of England*.

However, d'Indy was always prepared to come to earth when necessary, even if sometimes one finds it a little difficult to associate him with subjects like *L'Art et le Peuple* (1894) (a chorus for male voices), *Marche du 76e Régiment d'Infanterie* (1903) or *Sept Chants de Terroir* (1918) for piano duet. At the other end of the scale comes a charming little song, *La Première Dent* (1898)—but d'Indy was not attracted to or successful in this medium, any more than he was in that of the isolated piano " piece ".

He lived in a period whose early days did not produce a great deal of music acceptable to-day. In its time the *Poème des Montagnes* (1881), a Symphonic Poem for piano, was highly thought of. Reading it to-day reveals all the weaknesses of its time, and in spite of an interesting harmonic introduction, it must be regarded as more of a pioneer work than anything else, since it came at the period when Franck was encouraging the idea of providing the piano with a repertoire of large-scale works: later, Ravel was to work upon the same principle, which came to life in *Gaspard de la Nuit* (1908).

I do not think that *Wallenstein* is really a work for to-day, although its general outline and scope are of a quality which prevents its being entirely " dated ". On the other hand, *Le Chant de la Cloche* is worth performing because of its orchestral effects which for their time were remarkable and for the fact that such an approach is rare with d'Indy.

The first work which can be considered as in every way acceptable is the *Suite en ré dans le style ancien* (1886) for trumpet, two flutes and strings, largely because it is " dans le style ancien ", although in no sense mere *pastiche*, the style being more concerned with the quality of the movements than with a deliberate use of ancient harmonic processes. The titles, " Prélude ", " Entrée ", " Sarabande ", " Menuet ", " Ronde française ", connect with those of the late works, such as: the 'Cello Sonata (1924-1925)—" Entrée ", " Gavotte en Rondeau ", "Air ",

" Gigue "; Sextet (1927-1928)—" Ouverture, Entrée de sonate ", " Divertissement ", " Thème, Variations et Finale "; and the Trio for piano, violin and 'cello (1929)— " Entrée en sonate ", "Air ", " Courante ", " Gigue en rondeau sur une vieille chanson française ".

The three serious music dramas should find their places in the repertoire, particularly *L'Etranger*, which is in every way acceptable and practicable. *Fervaal* is rarefied, but its real obstacle lies in its vast scoring which is not an economic proposition. *La Légende de Saint-Christophe* presents difficulties in production because of its many scene changes but it is quite convincing and satisfying in concert performance. This vast work came just at the wrong moment, for by the time it was completed, music had definitely turned away from longevities and philosophies. Its reception was more than respectful and the work made a deep impression in spite of everything; but it was not of the style and idiom which, at that time, would ensure a strong following. Its message was several-sided but slightly repellent in its racial implications.

This very broad survey omits the vastly proportioned Violin Sonata (1903-1904) and *Souvenirs* (1906), the latter described as a " pièce pour orchestre ", an intensely personal and beautiful work which d'Indy hesitated to publish.

It is peculiar that one so deeply religious should have left so little organ music. The pieces extant, *Prélude et Petit Canon* (1893) and *Pièce en Mi Bémol* (1911), together with the *Vêpres du Commun des Martyrs* (1899) hardly contribute anything significant to the repertoire of the instrument to which their composer's teacher contributed so lavishly and splendidly.

In a large output it is often difficult to select a list fully representative of the composer which shows his progress while being acceptable to present-day standards. The reader may be recommended to study the choice made here, and the works will give him a clear insight into d'Indy's technical and musical ideals:

1. Wallenstein (1873-1881).
2. Le Chant de la Cloche (1879-1883).
3. Suite en ré dans le style ancien (1886).
4. Symphonie Cévenole (1886).
5. Fervaal (1881-1895).
6. " Istar " Variations (1896).
7. Second String Quartet (1897).
8. L'Etranger (1898-1901).
9. Second Symphony in B flat (1902-1903).
10. Violin Sonata (1903-1904).
11. Jour d'Eté à la Montagne (1905).
12. Souvenirs (1906).
13. Piano Sonata (1907).
14. La Légende de Saint-Christophe (1908-1915).
15. Poéme des Rivages (1919-1921).
16. Thème varié, Fugue et Chanson (1925).
17. Diptyque Méditerranéen (1925-1926).
18. Concerto for flute, piano, 'cello, and strings (1926).
19. Suite for flute, violin, viola, 'cello and harp (1927).
20. Sextet for two violins, two violas, and two 'cellos (1928).
21. Third String Quartet (1928-1929).
22. Trio en sol for piano, violin, and 'cello (1929).
23. Fantasie sur un vieil air de ronde français for piano (1930).

These twenty-three works from a total of 105 show

d'Indy's artistic growth and progress, at the same time indicating how closely knit were his ideals in precept and practice. It must be clearly understood, however, that exclusion from this list does not imply that the excluded are not worth playing and studying. The interested searcher will find many small gems among the songs, choral settings and piano pieces which will delight him, but which add nothing important to the d'Indy canon.

II. AESTHETIC

Although d'Indy was the apostle of classicism, he did not view romanticism askance; but he insisted that the sonata and symphony design should be rigidly adhered to. Anything romantic he welcomed as long as it was based upon classical and traditional processes. He could not regard a programmatic multi-movement orchestral work in any light but that of the Symphonic Poem. He never indulged in the search for sonorities for their own sake, and although he had a strong sense of orchestral colour, he regarded it merely as part and parcel of the technique. When he attempted landscape painting the result does not appear altogether happy; but this impression may originate in too close a regard of him as a classicist. However, there is not a very great deal of contrast between the objective works, and the technique is practically the same in each case—the openings of *Jour d'Eté à la Montagne* and the much later *Diptyque Méditerranéen* paint dawn in the same manner—a sustained veil of string tone through which an ever-increasing melodic contour worms its way (compare Ravel's *Daphnis et Chloé*; the theme winds up from the bass, but there is a lot of movement all round it). The content of d'Indy's two works is, naturally, different.

d'Indy had no objection to subjective or objective romanticism provided that it was portrayed through classical process and design. His strictures upon the Schola students in this regard were imposed because he considered effect for its own sake too easy a way of making music. His firm belief in tradition, his veneration for the later works of Beethoven and his admiration for Weber and Schumann (the latter qualified, it is true) had shown him that romanticism could be painted upon a classical foundation. His great ambition was that his pupils should write beautiful things, and this conception of beauty included formal balance, tonal relationship, and thematic opposition. The emotional content of the music, therefore, sprang from the music itself and lay in the rise and fall of the material.

d'Indy's music is always extremely easy to follow. His Gallic clarity allied to the classical ideal allowed only one thing at a time; consequently, there is not very much opportunity or occasion for " interpretation ". His scores are so well organised that whatever should stand out in relief does so of its own volition. His emphasis upon the architectural aspect of a work simply denotes that he insisted upon this approach rather than that of Impressionism or any pure baths of sound. Those who imagined that classicism spelt academicism naturally resented the imposition of it upon the then newly flowering French music. Further, d'Indy was a confirmed Wagnerite, although holding the opinion that the style and approach could not be assimilated into French Art. His Wagnerism, however, was not nearly as pronounced as his enemies liked to proclaim. He viewed Wagner as a great man who had solved the problem of symphonic music drama and who, in *Parsifal*, had composed a work which in its generality appealed to everything d'Indy held dear.

His championship of classicism, therefore, simply amounted to an insistence upon that type of technique as the basis for music of every kind. He was more concerned that French composers should write symphonies and symphonic music than that they should spend their time upon works which had little traditional authority. Nevertheless, he was not so hide-bound in this respect as to expect anything but that the material should decide the form, and not the form the material.

His aesthetic aimed at the use of classical design as the means of conveying beauty and expression. It was said of Franck that the discovery of one single new chord was sufficient to make him happy for a whole day. Of d'Indy it was said that the discovery of a strong constructivist basis sufficed to place a work upon the highest peak of excellence, regardless of the musical results. If this were true, d'Indy would have been nothing but a pedant, which, of course, was not the case.

III. TECHNIQUE

There are three types of d'Indy melody, the " long tune ", the quasi-" chanson populaire " and the fragment or cellule forming the origin of future material. Few composers of the generation had the art of writing the infinite type of melody (well-balanced, concise and perfectly if somewhat squarely organised) as highly developed as had d'Indy's teacher, Franck. It may be said that Franck is not always highly lyrical, but in those places where he let his fancy roam freely, he achieved a quality of lyricism which, in spite of the open way in which it is built, sounds perfectly spontaneous. This was the mainstay of his musical instinct. d'Indy rarely attempted to follow in Franck's footsteps, but when he did become lyrical, the construction is not so obvious, because the tune is not so long. d'Indy adopted this type of melody when writing Variations. Elsewhere, it is interesting to notice how he brings it into play when dealing with a

romantically pictorial subject. Even then it has none of
the suave range of his master. These linear themes of d'Indy
rely upon an extreme use of conjunct movement and an
equally extreme one of disjunct. He is either very, very
linear or very, very disjunct. However, he let his thought
move perfectly freely within whichever quality he was
thinking. It sometimes appears that he found any out-
burst of spontaneous lyricism rather outside his concept
of music. Whether this was all part and parcel of his
personal background is impossible to say, but it falls into
line with the normal restraint which he always practised in
everyday life. When free from inhibitions, he is invariably
very beautiful, but the tunes are not always distinguished in
themselves. One cannot describe him as a great melodist,
yet within the whole context of the work, one finds ineffably
lovely themes which gain their effect simply through the
treatment he metes out to them. We may take three
examples of such tunes at random:

Ex.5 *a)*   Piano Sonata

b)

c)   Jour d'été à la Montagne

d)   Concerto for Piano, Flute, Cello, with Strings

We shall examine the Sonata in full in due course: for the moment we content ourselves with noting the tranquillity and smoothness of this theme. Franck undoubtedly would have taken this line much further (d'Indy repeats it, slightly varied, and higher) and would have found some little point capable of forming the germ for another strain.

The second type of theme is one which is easy to adopt and which need not be of any great length. We quote three, noting that the first is a genuine " chanson populaire ":

This type of theme need not detain us. d'Indy works it more by repetition than by expansion, and this leads us directly to the third and most important type, for it forms one of the features by which d'Indy is recognisable.

This third type consists of short fragments of no significance in themselves, from which something of thematic importance grows as the work progresses. These cellules have some characteristic element about them, some very personal interval or rhythmic figure suggestive of many facets. The principle may be seen at its fullest development in the *Prélude, Choral et Fugue* of Franck, whose thematic content is undeniably traceable to one short figure, and in the *Prélude, Aria et Final*, which is formed entirely upon fragments of insignificant as well as of important material accumulating as the work proceeds. This particular manner is both cyclical and germinal. In several places the whole themes are quoted, slightly varied, this process applying the cyclical principle to the thought. Elsewhere, the condition is as I have stated. It would not be far wrong to note the similar germinal process forming the technique of Sibelius' Symphonies, but whether Sibelius is at all familiar with these works of Franck I cannot say.

d'Indy saw in it a perfectly natural and logical way of obtaining cohesion, whether the actual process is obvious to the listener or not. One of the most important marks which d'Indy left upon music was this cyclical and germinal technique which later composers have also adopted.

As an example of this, we may study certain aspects of the *Second String Quartet*, based upon a motto (in itself a Gregorian fragment) which Mozart thought of first in symphonic music when he wrote the finale to the " Jupiter " Symphony. That d'Indy borrowed it from Mozart is doubtful, knowing his opinion of that composer. Knowing also his innate religiosity and passion for Gregorian music, it is safe to assume that he took it from that source, possibly quite unintentionally. This Quartet shows a certain whimsical side of d'Indy's nature. The cellule is as follows and is printed in this somewhat enigmatical manner:

Ex.7

This very unpromising germ goes through a number of alterations; yet when it is directly presented it never sounds the same twice over. Here are a few ways in which d'Indy uses it:

Ex.8 a) b) c)

The cellule is both melodic and accompanimental, the whole work, therefore, being completely thematic. This is open to the objection that the Quartet is simply one varied movement. d'Indy maintained that the traditional design of such works was, indeed, fundamentally an organic whole, and viewed the matter as one work divided into several movements, none of which should or could be separable from the others. In the case of this Quartet, such cohesion is absolutely binding; in other works separate performance of movements is prevented by quotation of theme, making the divided situation musically unintelligible.

d'Indy never swerved in this approach to the symphonic principle. The very brevity of this next fragment, with its characteristic intervals, invites treatment by inversion,

in itself nothing very enterprising or original; but in many cases both inversion and retrogression do not sound convincing and appear to have been used simply for their own sake—another short cut, and a line of least resistance.

However, d'Indy showed that there was no reason why there should be only one cellule, and in his Symphony in B flat, a truly monumental work, he uses two, the second of which contains the complete d'Indy characteristic. (There are other themes which play important rôles in the work, but they are of a subsidiary character.)

The fact that Ex. 10A represents Evil and Ex. 10B Good need not concern us; the work is perfectly convincing without any knowledge of this spiritual battle and results in an ordinary symphonic conflict. Some of the ramifications through which the themes pass may be quoted:

Finally, they appear in the form of a magnificently triumphant Chorale which the ear realises to be the state at which the whole work has been aiming:

Ignoring formal considerations for the moment, this Symphony has a cohesion and continuity which fulfil all symphonic essentials, simply through the cyclical and germinal principles.

Similar examples can be found in all the other works, both orchestral and chamber. The use of the cellule, however, has given the impression in certain quarters that d'Indy lacked a spontaneous lyricism, and that, instead of an inspirational impulse, his large works are all constructed upon some kind of cerebral formula. This has arisen mainly because of his own insistence in his teaching, and he made a reputation for himself as an advocate of classical device and opponent of sound for its own sake for the fulfilment of any programmatic basis the work might have. One has but to look at d'Indy's programmatic works to see how similar was his mode of approach when writing them. Derivation, permutation and quotation were the bones and sinews of his thought, but he covered them with flesh. It will be seen that a cellule is not a theme in itself; this is often not clearly understood.

d'Indy was not very concerned with harmony for its own sake, preferring to regard it in the light of normal polyphonic occurrence, and to use it as a means of modulation. Never once did he attempt to show the younger generation that he could write in their harmonic idiom if he chose, and although he was one of the leaders of harmonic progress at the beginning of the twentieth century, he rarely, if ever, progressed further than a free use of the augmented triad— which is not going very far. His strong feeling for tonality was not directed by any attraction to necessitous tonal relations. He was not over-concerned with the succession of keys from dominant to dominant, and was happy to work in whatever key his thought naturally led him. It is true that he drew up an elaborate system of key application to the several characters and situations in *La Légende de Saint-Christophe*, but this was an extreme case, as far as I can make out.

Franck and d'Indy thought alike here. They both insisted upon tonality of some kind all the time, but laid down no arbitrary rule of process. Franck was obsessed with the key of F sharp, regarding it as the acme of light. d'Indy had no particular favourite key and he shed light upon his music by suddenly changing from one extreme to another. This next example gives the clue to his idea:

He was very fond of turning a tonic into a dominant:

The augmented triad d'Indy found useful as a means of impelling the music forward. There is a striking example in the Symphony in B flat, while the next example will show a similar attitude towards it, but one which does not have a forward effect:

Although the "-alities" left him unmoved, occasionally he got quite near them, and in a case like this

one can see the immediate difference in outlook between d'Indy who keeps the tonalities similar in each "hand" and Les Six who would have gone in contrary motion in similar quantities and qualities, but in opposing tonalities.

Generally speaking, d'Indy was not semitonal, but now and again he used an emotional harmony strongly redolent of Franck, like the following:

the succeeding treatment being typical of all the Franckian processes. This work, coming as it did (1925) when d'Indy was entering his final period and turning to early classicism, represents the last connection with the language of Franck.

d'Indy always treated rhythm freely, and although there are not many instances of careless rapture or of the serene lyricism of the infinite melody, his music is notable for its plasticity. This he learned from his study of Gregorian chant and his researches into its attendant variations. It is a commonplace to say that his rhythm is contained within the context and is not impinged for some special effect, for it stands to reason that a basically polyphonic composer thinks naturally in this manner. However, where d'Indy succeeded in one place where so many have failed was in the use of quintuple and septuple time. There are few composers capable of progressing really smoothly with no obvious division of the measure into **1**, 2, 3 **4**, 5 or **1**, 2, **3**, 4, 5 Holst is often convincing in these rhythms, but d'Indy appears to have discovered a real secret for evenness. This he achieved by the use of a triplet figure, usually from the fourth to the fifth beat. There is a good example in the last movement of the Symphony in B flat, and another:

Ex.18   Poème des Rivages

where the syncopation of the first three beats leaves the ear in doubt as to the moment of accentuation, the triplet moving the music smoothly to the next bar.

Septuple time he used very rarely. This quotation

Ex.19   Violin Sonata

demonstrates the potency of a short theme, too brief really for such a description. The piano part rhythmically alters the state of the first theme, quoted here:

It is more elastic when changed in mode:

Irregular barring was not a feature of d'Indy's technique, but the wayward feeling given by the following quasi-"chanson populaire" theme is obtained solely by such a process:

He was also perfectly flexible in his treatment of simple triple time, and over and over again the monotony of the triple rhythm is broken in this way, ♩ ♩ | ♩ ♩ not an exceedingly clever device but one which he and his disciples turned into a characteristic. He was rather fond of the rhythm ♫ ♫ ♫ | , which appears constantly, and in itself gives a jerk to the otherwise suave fluency of the music. These little characteristics he passed on to his pupils, not in any arbitrary manner but simply by his own example.

The finale of the Second String Quartet should also be studied in this connection. It is simply a reminder of the Beethoven " ritmo di tre battuto ", and the bar lines do not in any way interfere with each other or cause complexity and possible confusion.

d'Indy's free and supple rhythms are the elements which give life to his music, as, indeed, they must do to all music; but the results are obtained through means of omission—that is to say, any disturbing of the natural flow of the music gains its effect because it appears only occasionally. The over-use of spasmodic rhythmic explosions defeat their own purpose, and what should be singularly effective moments nearly become clichés.

Quintuple measures make an early appearance in his works, and he taught his Schola Cantorum pupils to accustom themselves to its sudden appearance in whatever music they might be playing. This can be seen in the *Treize Pièces Brèves* which he wrote as sight-reading tests for the *Cours du IIe degré*. These little pieces, the like of which are written every year in all conservatoires, suggest that the standard of sight-reading was very high. The compositions range from 1908 to 1915, the set commencing with a Cadenza for the Second Piano Concerto in A by John Christian Bach. Here are examples of what the student suddenly finds himself faced with:

Ex.23

There may be nothing at all complicated or difficult in these examples, but they are rather disturbing for the player under the circumstances, there being no time allowed for preliminary study, as the pieces were not designed as initiative tests.

IV. DESIGN

Considerable indication has been given in these pages of d'Indy's approach to the Sonata and Symphony and to what is loosely and misleadingly called " Sonata Form ", and there is no need to go into the matter again here, since so much of what has been said about the cyclical and germinal manner applies itself to formalistic matters. It would be quite wrong, however, to pass over the manner in which he excelled (as few others have excelled) and which he studied in the (late) works of Beethoven, Schumann, and Franck. This is the Variation Manner, which it is preferable so to describe rather than the more usual "Air (or Theme) and Variations " or " Variations upon a Theme " (of some sort, so often by some other composer). This manner is the easiest of all to deal with, given a reasonable amount of technical facility and disregard for the results. There are not a great number of composers who have succeeded in combining technical skill with musicality because of the tendency to emphasise the act of writing Variations for their own sake instead of using the design for an expressive purpose. The ordinary routine devices can be effected quite easily and there is no merit whatsoever in so doing. Any themes can be combined, inverted, " cancrizaned ", and what-you-will, if the composer does not mind how the devices sound when accomplished. This is pure cerebrality. It is a boast of the followers of Arnold Schoenberg (1874)—who deserves a better fate than to have attracted so many copyists —that all the classical devices of the early composers are at their disposal. Of course they are, and since the music is controlled entirely by a note-row or series, the aural effect is of no consequence at all, the result being purely " eye music ". The Variation Manner requires something more than a test of arbitrary skill, and even when the opposite school of thought is followed, there still remains something inevitable in the whole concept. One knows that sooner or later the theme will appear in triumph with the air of saying, as in Dukas' words, " Here I am; had you forgotten me? " d'Indy put forward an altogether individual solution to this problem, and his well-ordered mind went very much further than the mere act of writing a-Variation-a-day, thus compiling a series of short little pieces.

Those who regard him as lyrically deficient and feel that his music is entirely cerebral and lacking in any expressive feeling, should study the two great examples of his use of the Variation Manner—he wrote three such works, but the third is by no means great, although equally convincing.

The term " Symphonic Variations " implies a continuous flow of music from start to finish, with no pause between the Variations. d'Indy extended the whole conception and brought it within the scope of the Symphonic Poem, as did Richard Strauss in his *Don Quixote*. d'Indy did not describe different events, but he also wrote a little connecting link between each Variation (which the French indicate with the word *enchâiné*) having a distinct bearing upon the programme of the work—in itself a denial of his alleged dislike of programme music. However, still further than this,

d'Indy, by reason of the programme, inverted the whole
thing. The more involved Variations lead to the gradual
stripping down to the bare theme, and throughout, one is
listening to a work which is constantly unfolding instead of
accumulating.

I have analysed the *Istar* Variations very fully elsewhere,[1] but in a consideration of d'Indy one simply cannot
pass over the work by reference to another study of it.

The programme is taken from Chant VI of the Assyrian
Epic Poem of Idzubar. This poem describes how, in order
to liberate her lover from the nether regions, the Goddess
Istar has to pass through seven gates, divesting herself of
a jewel or article of apparel at each, so that she passes
through the last gate in triumphant nakedness. The principle
of composition is at once made clear; it may be an obvious
one, but d'Indy was the first and only one to think of it.

Two themes play an important rôle in the course of the
work, before the appearance of the main one. These
represent Istar knocking at each gate and then passing
through.

The first Variation is remarkable because it consists of the
harmonisation of the theme, without the theme itself.
d'Indy had done this earlier in the *Poèmes de Montagnes*

[1] *A Course in Musical Composition*, Part Two (Bosworth).

where there is an Introduction of this nature; but in this work it is merely a series of harmonic chordal progressions. In *Istar* the variation is perfectly satisfactory in itself—the semi-tonal wood-wind works against the string tremolandos, through which a sustained brass passage moves, the effect being almost musical impressionism.

During the course of the work there are several impassioned tunes, marked *bien chanté* (this was a favourite expression with d'Indy), which completely refute the charge that, in addition to eschewing a programme, d'Indy set his face against expressive feeling. The theme declares itself after an almost unbearably beautiful[1] string variation, which is followed by a triumphant connecting link; the theme is played in unison. The first bars connect it immediately with the motif described by d'Indy as " The Call " (Ex. 24A).

Ex. 25

d'Indy does not adhere to a tonic in this work, and the key range is wide and astonishing in its scope. This may be tabulated as follows, the " Call " and " March " being in the keys of their respective Variations:

Variation	One	. .	F
,,	Two	. .	E
,,	Three	. .	B flat
,,	Four	. .	F sharp (G) flat
,,	Five	. .	C
,,	Six	. .	A flat
,,	Seven	. .	D
Theme	.	. .	F

[1] I have used the same phrase as used by Philip Heseltine in respect to the string Variation in Delius' First Dance Rhapsody, *Delius* (The Bodley Head).

Each key underlines the prevailing mood of Istar at the moment, and, emphasised by the actual spirit and quality of the music goes through the gamut of human emotions.

This work remains one of the most imaginative and powerful of its kind. Some commentators have remarked upon it as " curiously inverted ", but there is nothing curious about it, once the programme has been studied.[1] d'Indy proclaimed himself a master of resource, and *Istar* can rank among the finest works of the century in its technical mastery, its logic, and its combination of technique and musical feeling.

This work was a foretaste of what he was to postulate in his later *Cours* at the Schola Cantorum. His Symphony in B flat laid down his symphonic principles; the Variation Manner, combined with the cyclical and germinal processes, received its crowning glory in the Piano Sonata.

d'Indy holds the honour of being only the second French composer to have written such a work[2]—it is a curious fact that the genre made no appeal to Saint-Saëns, who covered most fields; d'Indy's Sonata stands unique in its general design and layout, for it is an enormous set of Variations, the movements being absolutely inseparable. The work, nevertheless, falls into the traditional framework.

In this Sonata, d'Indy professes his artistic faith and the work serves as a practical justification of his pedagogic principles. Herein are found the highest expressions of a spiritual ideal, realised by means of a musical impulse which, at the same time, bears all the imprints of musical scholarship and consummate technique. This successful harnessing of all the elements which constitute great Art is an event which happens only too rarely, and the Sonata sets a standard for all others which strive after similar ends. In a study of this Sonata one is bound to emphasise the composer's workshop, and one hesitates before taking this plunge because

[1] Similar misunderstanding occurs over Ravel's *Bolero*.

[2] Paul Dukas was the first.

of the danger of giving false impressions. It is, unfortunately, necessary that the world's greatest music should be submitted to this kind of dissection, otherwise no lessons could be learnt from it; but words are not enough, and are certainly inadequate to give the whole picture of a composer's meaning. It is necessary, of course, to study and hear the work in question. Where d'Indy's great Sonata is concerned, opportunities for the latter are extremely rare. The work is described as " difficult "; one is rather weary of this cry, for all music is difficult, whether the difficulties be technical or inspirational. This Sonata presents no difficulties which a first-rate pianist cannot cope with; but the player must have a deep insight into the construction and philosophy of the work. In these days of hurry, pianists do not, alas, have unlimited periods for study. It is necessary for them to earn their daily bread, and this is not earned either in their studios or in the performance of music which claims concentrated listening on the part of the hearer, and I do not imply that this type of listening should be merely technical and analytical, for these are the least important calls upon a listener.

This Sonata provides an ideal for the composer since its logical cohesion is absolutely complete. It preaches no sermon, but it does reflect the mental ecstasy of one who is at peace with his God and with his fellow-men, and is fully conscious of his powers as he receives them from above. It is not necessary to express oneself upon the full orchestra to achieve this effect, although the greater part of the world's " great music " certainly does find its ultimate disclosure in this medium. This is not the eulogy of an enthusiast, written down in the heat of a moment; it is a result of some years' contemplation of the work itself. One can but exhort the reader to find it and judge for himself.

There is no programme here. The Sonata is a combination of technique and subjective feeling. It does indeed give the answer to those who feel that such subjectivity cannot depend

upon the classical designs for its expression, but must expand
itself freely and at length. Design (it is preferable to call
it that rather than " form ") is no restrictive framework.
It is simply a convenient way of sealing up the ideas into
a comprehensive and logical entity. It is in every way
pliable and plastic, and the composer subconsciously directs
the formal framework to fit in with his ideas. There is no
textbook implication in showing how this particular work is
made, and this does not suggest that d'Indy drew up a kind
of blue-print in advance, as certain other composers have
done—indeed, by the time he came to compose the Sonata
he thought instinctively in certain formalistic designs, and it
was as natural for him to express his ideas in this way as
to speak what is known as " good grammar " without
parsing his sentences in advance. However, that does not
preclude the reader and student of any work seeing the
nature of the construction and drawing a blue-print from the
deductions made in the course of study.

Unlike *Istar*, d'Indy puts his cards on the table at once.
There are three main themes which pervade the work, each
too long to be a cellule. These main materials are as follows:

Ex. 26A has already been quoted on page 57 and is repeated
here for convenience sake.

Of these, Ex. 26c makes its first appearance in the middle
of the first movement.

d'Indy commences with an introductory passage, binary in form, the whole being repeated and varied. The connection with the chief themes is easy to see:

Ex. 27

The first movement consists of four variations upon Ex. 27A, which may indeed be termed the theme of the work, the movement ending with a perfectly open presentation of the theme *mutatum*, as d'Indy himself puts it. The first appearance of this theme, which falls into ternary form, is heavenly music, full of philosophical dignity and tranquillity.

Ex. 27B is used as a link between the Variations, as in *Istar*, its last three notes forming the material of the second Variation, in this manner,

which is redolent of Franck. It turns out during the course
of the section that Part Two of Ex. 27A is really the original
state of the link, inverted. At the end of this Variation, the
link itself is presented in triple time, thus:

It joins Variations Three and Four in much the same
manner.

Variation Four initiates the third element of the work,
Ex. 27C, over a running left-hand part. Ex. 27B plays a
rôle in the main flow of the music and Ex. 27A and Ex. 27C
find themselves in combination, in this manner:

The final presentation of the theme of the work is har-

monised in a manner different from the original, for while its
first state was in E minor, its second is in E major, and the
original mental calm takes on a spirit of resignation in the
change of modality. The writing is chordal, as in the first
statement. There are supremely lovely pages in this movement.

In design the second movement, representing the Scherzo,
is perfectly normal, and has two Trios. For the sake of
clarity we quote the original condition of the material in each
case. The Scherzo itself finds its origin in the link (Ex. 27B)

expressed in the pianism in this way:

The first Trio derives from 27C:

the second from **27B**:

Ex.34

The Coda is based upon the idea of a second Trio.

The third movement (the Finale) is in First Movement design, with Introduction. This opens in the same way as does the whole Sonata, but instead of passing to the link theme, a new one appears, which will play some important rôles as the movement proceeds:

Ex.35

There is a good deal of measured bravura writing before the movement proper begins, and this, again, uses new material:

Ex.36

as does the connecting episode:

Ex. 37

It may be thought at this point, and with some justification, that the claim of the work to be built upon three themes
falls to the ground; but such a claim should surely not
preclude something subsidiary somewhere, provided that the
main material only makes a constructional appearance in the
stream of the music. In the present case, the two themes
of the Finale are an intrusion and represent an alien element
imposing itself, uninvited. The second subject pulls the link
back into place in contour if not in actual interval.

Ex. 88

In the course of the development section, Ex. 34, which
originally played a subsidiary part in the Introduction to the
movement, appears in an interesting manner.

Ex. 39

The closing Coda displays the main theme over some
bravura pianism.

This is not triumphant, and it goes to no higher dynamic than forte. However, when it reaches the third section of its ternary condition, it appears treble forte in combination with the intruder (Ex. 36)

which in the closing quiet bars assumes a state of regeneration, as it were, and is followed by the second subject, in this way:

Blanche Selva sees in this another conquest of Good over Evil, the latter being entirely transfigured, with its basic qualities eliminated.[1] This is a trifle fanciful.

[1] *La Sonate* (Rouart-Lerolle).

As I have said, to analyse this great music in this cold manner conveys nothing of its warmth and humanities. The work displays the Sonata style in all its essentials and represents the acme of Vincent d'Indy's achievement in its particular manner. It is thoroughly convincing in both technique and aesthetic.

d'Indy's later *Theme varié, Fugue et Chanson* shows no lessening of skill, but the work is not entirely individual as it is too strongly redolent of Franck; this was doubtless instinctive, and it forms d'Indy's farewell to the manner of his great teacher. The same processes are to be found, the variations being linked together by a short figure. The pianism is altogether simpler than in the Sonata, and pianists of quite moderate ability will find it well within their scope. It is well worth playing and offers no mental puzzles for its understanding.

This consideration of d'Indy's musical " make-up " has, of necessity emphasised the processes. The ultimate proof of all Art is its realisation, and in music the only way in which this can be achieved is by playing it and listening to it. d'Indy has been coupled too indivisibly with Franck. Although there is at times an harmonic affinity between the two composers, d'Indy does not actually resemble Franck in any way except that of Ideal. He was not a mere copyist. The relationship between the Franckists is perfectly clear, and they form an interesting group on their own. The resemblances are mainly those of process; in material, they are subtly as well as patently different.

In another medium d'Indy played a particularly important part in the history of music and directly influenced a complete culture.

d'Indy and the Lyric Stage

D'INDY's contribution to the lyric stage is of the highest importance, for nothing like the scope and substance of the three great works had up to that time emanated from any French composer. The idea of " symphonic opera " indivisible into arias and ensemble numbers, with no recitatives, sprang from Wagner, of course, and like him d'Indy achieved his works in terms of music, managing to carry those moments of incidental conversation along with its flow. This concept, together with a certain number of fragmentary themes which appear and reappear constantly as occasion demands, immediately gained for him the opprobrium of those who imagined that he was trying to impinge Wagnerism upon Gallic Art. This charge of Wagnerianism had already been laid at the door of Gounod, Bizet and Massinet without the slightest foundation upon fact. In the case of d'Indy, there were certain points which indicated a contact and an influence, but these were more general than particular. d'Indy's fragments, however, are always more impersonal than clearly personal and they act as cellules and not as " visiting cards ". d'Indy's admiration of Wagner did not blind him, and he did not consider that the concept was one which could be allied entirely to Gallic thought. Debussy remarked that, actually, there was very little of Wagner in d'Indy when one examined a work like *L'Etranger*. The similarity lay in the metaphysical approach of both composers to their subjects, the pointing of an ideal and a moral, and also in the fact that d'Indy, like Wagner, wrote his own texts. d'Indy did so because he saw the absolute cohesion of the process, but it is hardly a significant connection; however, no one else at the time was doing it, for everyone applied to the hacks, who purveyed their wares in this field to any composer happening to want an opera libretto.

d'Indy did not go out of his way to please his audiences. The thought that possibly they would not want to be preached at never entered his head, for he was impelled to the works simply by an ardent creative desire.

His two " light " operas have made no impression, as might be expected. *Attendez-moi sous l'Orme* (1876-1882) was produced in order to gratify a wealthy patron, so we are led to understand,[1] while *Le Rêve de Cinyras* (1922-1923), enchanting music though it is, after its initial *succès d'estime*, faded out of the repertoire for more than one reason. This particular work holds much the same position in d'Indy's output as that held by Roussel's *La Testament de ma tante Caroline* (1932-1933), both being written " for fun " and as a relaxation from the more serious works which up to those moments had occupied both composers.

d'Indy's first dramatic work was not intended for the stage, but when *Le Chant de la Cloche* was performed at the Thêâtre de la Monnaie, Brussels, in 1912, it was found to form a parallel with Berlioz' *The Damnation of Faust*, neither work having been composed with stage production in mind. To-day we see a continuation of this operatic oratorio in Honegger's *Jeanne d'Arc au bucher*.

Le Chant de la Cloche is described as a Symphonic Legend, its text being taken from Schiller. Wilhelm, a master founder, is about to complete a magic bell of his own design, which will immortalise him. Feeling the approach of death, he invokes before him all the events of his life which have

[1] *Vincent d'Indy*, Léon Vallas (Albin Michel).

been associated with bells—baptism, love, fire, passion, and one particular night when the Dream Spirits came to him in the belfry, accompanied by his wife Lénore. His colleagues and acquaintances are eaten up with jealousy and spread the rumour that a bell of such a unique pattern, and constructed in the face of all set rules, cannot possibly be stable. A Priest announces that Wilhelm is dead. The cortège crosses the Square to the sound of the " In Paradisum ". Suddenly the new bell begins to toll, the others in the city responding in sympathy.

This nutshell synopsis will give some indication of the musical possibilities and d'Indy for the only time in his life indulged in the research after sonorities for their own sake, in the bell effects with which he loads his score. The music is very much of its period, of course, but it forms a landmark, as nothing of its nature and calibre had appeared in France since *The Damnation of Faust* and Franck's *Les Béatitudes*. It is exceedingly dramatic and would stand performance to-day with ease. d'Indy himself viewed it in places with disfavour during his later years, seeing in it traces of his early admiration of Meyerbeer, who had appeared to him to be the dramatic composer *par excellence* which, of course, he was—in his own way. *Le Chant de la Cloche* set the seal on d'Indy's reputation as a composer with a future. Indeed, his fame even at that early age (thirty-two) far exceeded that of his master. It represents a technique and aesthetic far in advance of its period and surroundings. Certain melodic twists which were to become a characteristic of d'Indy make their appearance here.

The first actual opera, music drama, "Action musicale " —whichever you will—was *Fervaal* (composed between 1881 and 1895), founded upon some music written for an earlier and uncompleted opera, *Axel*. The subjects of both works are Scandinavian in origin, but d'Indy transferred *Fervaal* to his native Cevennes. *Fervaal* was composed at the time of the revelation of *Parsifal*, which came to d'Indy while on a pilgrimage to Bayreuth, where, in company with his friend and fellow-student, Pierre de Bréville, he met both Wagner and Liszt. *Fervaal* has been called the " French Parsifal ", but such soubriquets are rarely convincing. The work was the biggest and most serious achievement in French opera up to its time. It covered a range of expression, postulated symphonically, which no previous French composer and, indeed, none outside Wahnfried, had achieved.

Fervaal, sole descendant of the primitive race of the Néuus, has been brought up by an old Druid named Arfgaard. An oracle has ordained that Fervaal shall reign supreme over the land of Cravann, provided that he remains chaste and ignorant of human love. He falls a victim to the beauty of a woman, Guilhen. Arfgaard rescues him from the woman, who immediately invades Cravann at the head of an army. Fervaal is defeated, and remembers his prophesied future. An old goddess, Kaito, tells him that the new life will be born out of death. Fervaal at once offers himself as a sacrifice to the knife of Arfgaard. At the crucial moment the voice of Guilhen is heard calling for help from the mountains. Fervaal kills Arfgaard and Guilhen dies of cold in the hero's arms. Carrying the dead woman, Fervaal climbs into the clouds, through which breaks the first ray of the sun, representing an ideal.

For this work d'Indy uses an enormous orchestra whose size is sufficient to militate against economic production, for there is no extravagance and nothing can be " cued-in " or omitted. Isolated in this way as it is, in d'Indy's catalogue, it is worth chronicling the wind required, which the reader may care to compare with similar-size orchestras of composers such as Richard Strauss and Josef Holbrooke:

4 Flutes	4 Bassoons
2 Piccolos	4 Saxophones
3 Oboes	4 Horns
Cor Anglais	4 Trumpets

4 Clarinets	8 Saxhorns
Bass clarinet	4 Tenor trombones
Double bass clarinet	Bass tuba

"Cornet à Bouquin" (a species of mountain horn).

This large orchestra not only reflects the influence of the study of Berlioz' *Instrumentation* but forms the practical proof of his complete knowledge of orchestral instruments as discussed in the *Cours*.

The general tone of the music draws the dividing line between sacred and profane. The texture is thick, but never obscure. In many places d'Indy seems to have remembered the March of the Knights in *Parsifal*, but never does he reach the pit of that commonplace melody for, above all, he regarded the singers' music as pre-eminent and refrained from hanging their words on to a vocal line devised from the orchestral texture. There is a certain sweetly cloying semi-tonalism which justifies itself through its quality of tenderness. A few bars of choral writing will illustrate this, and also the freedom with which he "crossed the parts":

The work is lyrical and symphonic and there are many magnificent moments. The only section which offers really satisfactory separation from the whole is the beautiful Prelude to Act One, which follows the Prologue;[1] this has been played many times at concerts in this country. It flows gently and easily in even quaver movement and its surface is entirely unruffled. The semitonalism I have mentioned can be illustrated instrumentally by passages such as these— notice the wide leap, a characteristic of d'Indy linear melody:

[1] Others are available and would stimulate interest, but no more, since they are incomplete in this form. Personally, I am inclined to deprecate extracts from symphonic operas.

d'Indy explains the process of thought underlying the composition of this work in Part Three of the *Cours*, tabulating it thus:

Act I (A)		Act 2 (B)		Act 3 (A)	
Scene 1	{ Religion Country	Scene 1	{ Religion Oracle	Scene 1	{ Religion Sacrifice
2	Love	2	War	2	Love and Death
3	War	3	{ Prophecy of Victory	3	{ Victory Light

In this way he endeavours to show some kind of ABA design. At the same time he applies certain keys to certain situations and emotions—A flat minor represents Unrest, Grief, Disturbed Dreams; D, Love, Everlasting Light, etc. One may say that this is convincing only to the mind which imagined it, and d'Indy cannot be gainsaid.

He admits the use of leitmotives, but states that they are used in the same way as used by Debussy in *Pelléas et Mélisande* whose composition followed that of *Fervaal*. This is a generous attitude under the circumstances and removes any idea that Debussy found the application in *Fervaal*. While trying to write in the declamatory style of Monteverde, d'Indy wishes everything to be sung—he had a horror of recitative. There are seven fundamental and seventeen accessory themes, none of them being of more than two or three bars, but from them the music gains its symphonic growth and the leitmotives fulfil the functions of cellules.

We give three more examples to show the type of technique which d'Indy used at the time of the composition of *Fervaal*:

The Franckian influence is discernible in these; but the influence of a teacher is usually apparent in the pupils and, bearing in mind the tremendous advance upon his contemporaries which Franck's technique and musical language demonstrated, it is not to be wondered at that the "new music" as expressed by Franck should have made its mark upon his symphonic admirers.

Fervaal gives the answer to those who maintain that d'Indy's music has no humanism or personal feeling. Such

7

a theory is easily refutable, but once such a reputation has gained a footing, it is often difficult to disprove it. d'Indy's insistence upon classical device brought this into assumption and caused much misunderstanding of his aesthetic, a misunderstanding quickly seized upon by his opponents. There is infinitely more human feeling in the classicism of d'Indy than in the neo-classicism of Camille Saint-Saëns.

Once more d'Indy went through a certain repudiation owing to the Meyerbeerian influence, but where this appears is impossible to discover, unless it be in the particular manner of writing for certain instruments. *Fervaal* remains a great work, but its future will always be dependent upon its requirements.

This is not the case with *L'Etranger*, which followed between 1898 and 1901. This work contains some of the most magnificent sea music in existence, and finds its parallel in this respect with *The Flying Dutchman* and Holbrooke's *Dylan*. It is scored for ordinary full orchestra, and requires singers with powerful voices; but they are never swamped by the orchestra. Of the three great music dramas of d'Indy, *L'Etranger* is at once the most equal, the most dramatic and the most acceptable to-day. Its Wagnerism lies mainly in the soaring soprano rôle. The texture of this work is remarkably slight. The music is more diatonic than that of *Fervaal* and, consequently, infinitely stronger. In this case, separation is possible, and one can envisage a stirring concert performance of Act Two, Scene 2, between Vita and the Stranger and also of the Symphonic Introduction to that act.

The story is not involved. A mysterious stranger appears in a fishing village. He is seen by Vita, who, alone of the villagers, does not view him with suspicion. Vita is betrothed to a young Customs Official. She enters into conversation with the Stranger and falls in love with him. The Stranger finds himself not insensible to Vita; this disturbs him, for he is on a Heavenly mission. He possesses a precious stone which originally had been fixed to the prow

of the ship belonging to Lazarus; this stone gives the
Stranger control of the sea.   The Customs Official tells Vita
that he has captured a smuggler and that his share of the
reward will enable them to get married. Vita is not interested.
The next day (Sunday) is stormy, but the Stranger prepares
to depart. Vita stands on the shore. She begs the Stranger
to remain, and asks him his name. He replies: " I have no
name.   I am he who loves, he who dreams, loving the poor
and oppressed, dreaming of the goodness of mankind. I
have walked across the world." As he has been conquered
by human passion, he must leave the village. He gives Vita
the ring, and leaves her. Vita sings an ardent invocation
to the sea and casts the ring into it. The storm gathers. A
fishing boat is seen to be in difficulties, but no one is brave
enough to go to the rescue—except the Stranger.   Vita
insists on going with him. They enter the sea, which
momentarily quietens down. The watchers are full of hope,
but suddenly an enormous wave sweeps up the shore,
engulfing all on the sea.   A fisherman intones the *De
Profundis.*

A few bars from the closing portion of Act One will indicate
the strength of music which characterises this work:

Ex.46

This surge of wonderful sound, Wagnerian (possibly), if only from the point of view of effect, contains the elements of what is known as great music. It does not rant, but conveys its meaning in a perfectly direct and unaffected manner.

In contrast, an interesting chorus may be noted which takes on the air of a " chanson populaire " and a " village en fête ":

Ex. 47

There are a number of fragmentary themes which appear from time to time, but not as many as in *Fervaal*. They form the basis of wonderfully clear, inspired and sincere music. Debussy was thrilled by it and one can see its influence in his *La Mer*, not from any thematic point of view, but in the general manner of portraying the sea in music. These two diametrically opposed aesthetics, therefore, became united in this instance, and, with certain other observations which the student of Debussy is forced to make, indicates that possibly Debussy was really drawn to this concept of music (his String Quartet is cyclical), but fought against it in order to form his own particular aesthetic. This is debatable, but none the less reasonable.

d'Indy uses the chorus in the *coulisses* as a quasi-orchestral entity, and at the end of the work, when the village folk are gathered at the water's edge, directs that they should have their backs to the audience in order that the voices may appear to come both from the stage (themselves) and from the *coulisses* (the sea). *Fervaal* concludes with the " Pange lingua ". *L'Etranger* ends with a man's voice reciting the first line of the *De Profundis*, the second line being taken up by the chorus. In the former, therefore, the religious element is spiritual and metaphysical; in the latter, it is purely personal and literal.

L'Etranger was criticised whole-heartedly for certain constructional features in the libretto. This has always happened and signifies nothing except that the critic feels that he could have done better himself. *L'Etranger* is not monumental because it puts forward no novel musical or philosophical problems and as yet has not influenced a great number of composers. It does not say the last word either in its period or for all time. *L'Etranger* is none the less a great music drama. It set a standard for French opera which only a great French composer could attempt to approach. That none has as yet done so, as far as can be made out, suggests that the time is not yet actually ripe. However, that time is coming; it is not far distant, and the rising generation will surely witness it, once the present craving for originality-at-all-costs has died a natural death.

d'Indy's third stage work, *La Légende de Saint-Christophe* (1908-1915), described as a " Drame sacré ", offers many problems whose complex nature cannot be solved between the two covers of one score. Here are found polemics of philosophy, metaphysics, racial prejudice and theology. Into this work he put all his loves and hates, and covered them with no veneer of sweet reason or toleration. The main trouble with *La Légende* is that it attempts too much and is too vast. Its production must be lavish and costly, while the constant changes of scene (at the first performance, at any rate) entail intervals of undue length. That is one reason why I described it as so satisfactory in the concert-hall.[1]

The story is based upon the legend by Jacques de Voragine and is as complex as such medieval legends can be. The giant, Auferus, decides to put himself at the disposal of the most powerful sovereign in the world, whoever he may be. First, he finds the Queen of Pleasure, who dwells in a species of Venusberg. There he comes into contact with the King of Gold, whose riches enable him to buy the Queen and everything she owns. Auferus decides that gold is the most powerful sovereign, and changes his allegiance. The King of Gold finds himself faced with Sathanäel, Prince of Evil, who proceeds to liquefy the gold. Auferus now sees that evil is the most powerful element in the world. Sathanäel shows his new subject the armies of sin, false doctrine, false prophets and false artists who have one common hate, that of Christ and Christian charity. These figures pass a belfry upon which a cross shines in the sunlight and stands out against the horizon. Sathanäel and the cloudy retinue are melted by the light of the cross and die, cursing the King of Heaven. Auferus at once transfers his attentions to this new King who has revealed himself through the Cross.

Then follows the Symphonic Prologue to the Second Act, known as " la Queste de Dieu ", which describes Auferus' travels and enquiries as to where he can find this new Sovereign. He visits all the kings of the earth and the leaders of armies, who tell him in turn that they are not he whom he seeks. He goes to Rome and asks the same question of the Pope, who gives the same answer, but adds: " When the pines of the forests bear white roses, then the King of Heaven will reveal himself to you." Auferus, not understanding this, returns to his native country. A hermit invites him to look for God in his heart and teaches him the three Christian virtues, Faith, Hope, and Charity, suggesting that he uses his strength by carrying people across the raging torrent which passes the hermit's cave. Auferus refuses

[1] Pages 8 and 52.

to help a lover, a merchant, and an emperor (who remind him of his old masters), but carries a child over. A tempest blows up; the child tells Auferus not to be dismayed, but to walk boldly onwards. " Do not be astonished, for it is I who created the world." The storm passes and Auferus sees that the pine stick he had been carrying bears white roses. The Child, Jesus, whom he had been carrying, baptises him with the name of Christopher and tells him to preach the faith all round the world.

Eventually Christopher is thrown into prison and condemned to death, in spite of the miracles he has wrought and the popularity he has found. The King of Gold, now Christopher's chief judge, is visited by the Prince of Evil, who demands a soul, either that of the King of Gold, the vilest, or that of Christopher, the noblest. The Queen of Pleasure comes to Christopher in his cell, in all her dazzling voluptuousness. Christopher prays for strength; through his prayers, divine grace touches the temptress, and the two join in a hymn to the glory of God. The next day is set for Christopher's execution. The crowd in the market place is immense. Christopher appears, singing. All through the preliminary tortures he continues his hymn to God, and after his head has been struck off, the song still rises to Heaven.

The Queen of Pleasure, purified by the blood of the Martyr, has become the Saint Nicea. She exhorts the crowd to practise charity, and the curtain falls with the invocation, " Saint Christopher, pray for us ".

d'Indy regarded this work more in the nature of a medieval "mystère" than in that of a music drama. The nine tableaux are presented in the manner of a series of pictures by Fra Angelico—indeed, in order to put himself in the framework of the story, d'Indy decorated the walls of his study with reproductions of the story, these being the only decorations in an otherwise austerely furnished room. The characters in Act One represent the types he abominated —bogus " savants " and financiers whose sole aim in life is to make money at the expense of other people.   Unlike Fervaal, Auferus (Christopher) remains pure and unsullied, and temptation does not seem to trouble him in the way that it troubled the Stranger.

The music is deeply felt and closely wrought.   A tonal scheme similar to that of *Fervaal* and *L'Etranger* is applied, but even more rigorously than in the first case.   *La Légende de Saint-Christophe* was the work of d'Indy's life, and into it he put all his musical and moral ideals.

The subject being basically religious, one is not surprised to find examples of Gregorian chant as cellules for the symphonic stream.   Here I must disagree fundamentally with M. Léon Vallas' theory that the use of these themes proves d'Indy's poverty of melodic invention.   The principle is no different from that of using the folk-song, and while there are many who feel that composers should not utilise any melodies but their own, it is conceded that the folk-song is a legitimate basis for musical thought, provided that it is modal and in keeping with the theme.   The subject of *La Légende* is one which calls for some religious musical expression, and it is preferable that d'Indy used genuine Gregorian cellules instead of writing pastiche.   d'Indy had given evidence of lyricism in previous works and the use of these fragmentary themes is simply another approach to that quality.   There is no possible objection to the Gregorian fundamental in this work since it is all part and parcel of the idea.   The cellule not being a theme in itself, it is easy to watch the symphonic growth from its root, and d'Indy is able to draw a lot from that little which increases in intensity according to the accumulative progress of the story.

Three examples of the Gregorian cellule may be seen on the following page:

Ex. 49 shows how d'Indy derives a main cellule upon a Gregorian basis and joins it to an ordinary one when the orchestra enters with the theme representing the crowd's admiration for the courage of Saint Christophe:

Other cellules bear this quasi-modal atmosphere, but the rest are diatonic and characteristic, especially that applicable to the High Court Judge, which d'Indy describes with the word " Meyerbeer "—this idol had tumbled to the ground many years earlier.

This work is splendidly characterised. d'Indy, unlike his teacher, was not nonplussed when it came to delineating Evil, and the First Act is excellent in this respect. The closing scene of the martyrdom of Saint Christopher is compelling in its suggestiveness without being theatrical. The general planning is original. Each scene is " announced " by an Historian and this condenses what otherwise would result in a work of too prodigious a magnitude.

There is only the Symphonic Interlude representing " La Queste du Dieu " which can be separated from the whole. This Interlude is extremely clear in its definition of question and answer, this lying in the short thematic link which joins the several travels of Auferus; in some respects one can see here an echo of the earlier " enchâiné " and link of *Istar*. The technique has a surprising freshness and vigour and the complete atmosphere is one of sincerity. *La Légende de Saint-Christophe* is one of those few works which, in the words of Vaughan Williams, " damned well had to be written ".

These three great works are dormant for the moment, but they will return to the repertoire when the world has come out of its present state of imbecility, when ideals once more take the place of tastes, and the hidden verities are re-sought.

★

d'Indy's music takes hold of its performers. The tide is flowing in his direction again, for the world needs a stable musical figure. The stability of Sibelius has played its part; now it is time to look for another, and he will be found not in an experimental atmosphere, but in that of romanticism founded upon classicism. The austerities of the neo-classicists are becoming increasingly boring, and musicians are beginning to crave for a little warmth and human feeling. There is every likelihood of d'Indy being

" discovered " as having all the essential qualities and quantities. It is significant that many so-called " ultra-moderns " speak of him with respect and regard, and in terms they do not apply to his immediate predecessors and contemporaries.

All highly stylised music dates, although this is not necessarily a sign that it is outmoded and, therefore, unacceptable; it merely implies that one can place the music within the framework of a certain period or periods. d'Indy is not in any way stylised; his language is universal, for his mannerisms are those of content and not of technique. He is being approached rather in reverse through his pupil Roussel,[1] whose thought found its impulse in the musical and idealistic approach of Vincent d'Indy.

d'Indy kept the symphonic principle alive when the mass of " -isms " and " -alities " were cluttering up the music of the 1920's. To-day, composers of all cultures use the cyclical and germinal processes, and modern symphonies can often be commended for their thematic cohesion and formalistic strength. This is the direct result of the teaching and example of Vincent d'Indy. When the day comes for France once more to lead the *avant-gardé*, it will be found that d'Indy and Roussel supply the new foundations, the former with his formalistic and moral forces, the latter with his harmonic and polyphonic astringencies, which emanate from the teaching of d'Indy. A direct line of stable symphonic impulse will thus be established, and instead of looking to Germany and Austria for authority, the world will find it in France. Already Milhaud (1892) and Honegger (1892) have established the d'Indy-Roussel principles, and Messiaen (1908) and Martinet (1912) are proclaiming that new thought which is traceable to Vincent d'Indy.

---

[1] Yet in *Debussy* (" Master Musicians ", Dent), Mr. Edward Lockspeiser states that d'Indy (among others) has had no " outstanding followers ".

APPENDIX A

LIST OF COMPOSITIONS

THIS is a rearrangement of the excellent chronological catalogue printed at the end of Léon Vallas' two-volume book on d'Indy. I have omitted several works which were planned but never carried into effect, those commenced and not completed, and those destroyed. The French titles and descriptions have been used; this, I know, is open to objection in an English book, but it is better than bi-linguality.

UNPUBLISHED WORKS

Sonate pour Piano	1870
Symphonie en la	1870-1872
Symphonie—" Jean Hunyade "	1874-1876
Ouverture—"Antoine et Cleopatre "	1876
Cantata—" Pour l'Inauguration d'Une Statue" (Baryton, Chœur et Orchestre)	1894
Ode à Valence (Soprano et Chœur)	1897
Musique de Scéne—" Veronica "	1920
" Two Scholars' Songs " (Two Voices)	1921
Chanson pour Deux Voix en forme de canon (Soprano et Baryton)	1931
Chant de Nourrice (Chœur pour trois Voix égales)	1931

Le Forgeron   1931
    (Chœur pour trois Solistes avec Quatuor à
    Cordes)

" Le Vengeance du Mari "   1931
    (Trois Solistes avec Chœur et Orchestre)

Dramatic Works

"Attendez-moi sous l'Orme "—Opéra-Comique
    (Enoch)   1876-1882
" Le Chant de la Cloche "—Légende dramatique[1]
    (Hamelle)   1879-1883
" Fervaal "—Action musicale (Durand)   1881-1895
" L'Etranger "—Action musicale (Durand) 1898-1901
" La Légende de Saint-Christophe "—Drame
    sacré (Rouart-Lerolle)   1908-1915
" Le Rêve de Cinyras "—Comédie musicale
    (Rouart-Lerolle)   1922-1923

Orchestral Works

Ballade-Symphonie—" La Forêt enchantée "
    (Heugel)   1878
Trois Ouvertures Symphoniques—" Wallenstein "
    (Durand)   1873-1881

       1. Le Camp
       2. Max et Thécla
       3. Le Mort de Wallenstein

Légende—" Sangefleurie " (Hamelle)   1884
Sérénade et Valse—Petit Orchestre (Hamelle) 1887
Suite (Six Pièces)—"Tableaux de Voyage "
    (Leduc)   1891

---

[1] I have included this fine work here because it was proved to have dramatic power when produced at the Théâtre de la Monnaie, Brussels, in 1912.

Variations Symphoniques—" Istar " (Durand) 1896

Divertissement " Chansons et Danses "—Instruments à vent (Durand) 1898

Deuxiéme Symphonie en si bémol (Durand) 1902-1903

Trois Pièces—" Jour d'Eté à la Montagne " (Durand) 1905

Pièce—" Souvenirs " (Durand) 1906

Sinfonia Brevis—" De Bello Gallico " (Rouart-Lerolle) 1916-1918

Suite Symphonique—" Poème des Rivages " (Rouart-Lerolle) 1919-1921

Diptyque Méditerranéen (Rouart-Lerolle) 1925-1926

Solo Instruments and Orchestra

Lied (Hamelle) 1884
    (Violoncelle et Orchestre)

Suite en ré dans le Style Ancien (Hamelle) 1886
    (Trompette, deux Flutes et Instruments à Cordes)

Symphonie sur un Chant Montagnard Français (Hamelle) 1886
    (Orchestre et Piano)

Fantaisie sur des Thèmes Populaires Français (Durand) 1888
    (Hautbois principal et Orchestre)

Concert (Rouart-Lerolle) 1926
    (Flute, Violoncelle, Piano et Orchestre à Cordes)

Chamber Music
A. Strings

1er Quatuor en ré (Hamelle) 1890

2er Quatuor en mi (Durand) 1897

Quintette (Senart)   1924
    (Deux Violons, Alto, et Violoncelle)

Sextuor (Heugel)   1928

3er Quatuor en ré bémol (Heugel)   1928-1929

B. Accompanied Chamber Music

Quatuor en la (Durand)   1878-1888
    (Piano, Violon, et Violoncelle)

Trio en sol (Rouart-Lerolle)   1929
    (Piano, Clarinette et Violoncelle)

Trio en sol (Rouart-Lerolle)   1929
    (Piano, Violon et Violoncelle)

C. Wind Instruments

Sarabande et Menuet (Durand)   1918
    (Flute, Hautbois, Clarinette, Cor et Basson)

Suite (Rouart-Lerolle)   1927
    (Flute, Violon, Alto, Violoncelle et Harpe)

SONATAS

Petite Sonate dans la Forme Classique—Piano
    (Hamelle)   1880

Sonata en ut—Violon et Piano (Durand)   1903-1904

Sonate en mi—Piano (Durand)   1907

Sonate en ré—Violoncelle et Piano (Rouart-
    Lerolle)   1924-1925

PIANO

Trois Romances dans Paroles (Schott)   1870

Poème Symphonique—"Poème des Montagnes"
    (Hamelle)   1881

Quatre Pièces (Hamelle)   1882
    1. Sérénade
    2. Choral grave
    3. Scherzetto
    4. Agitato

Trois Valses—" Helvétia " (Hamelle)   1882
    1. Aarau
    2. Schinznach
    3. Laufenburg
Nocturne (Hamelle)   1886
Promenade (Hamelle)   1887
Trois Pièces—" Schumanniana " (Hamelle)   1887
Treize Pièces—" Tableaux de Voyage " (Leduc) 1889
Menuet sur le Nom de Haydn (Durand)   1909
Treize Pièces Brèves (Henn)   1908-1915
Douze Petites Pièces Faciles (Henn)   1908-1915
Trois Albums—" Pour les Enfants de Tous
    Ages " (Rouart-Lerolle)   1919
Thème varié, Fugue et Chanson (Rouart-
    Lerolle)   1925
Suite—" Contes de Fée " (Rouart-Lerolle)   1925
Six Paraphrases sur des Chansons enfantines de
    France (Heugel)   1928
Fantaisie sur un Vieil Air de Ronde (Heugel) 1930

PIANO DUETS

Petite Chanson Grégorienne (Schola Cantorum) 1904
Sept Chants de Terroir (Rouart-Lerolle)   1918

SONGS

Attente—Victor Hugo (Hamelle)   1872-1876
Madrigal—Robert de Bonnières (Hamelle)   1872-1876
Plainte de Thécla—Robert de Bonniéres
    (Hamelle)   1880
La Chevauchée du Cid—Robert de Bonnières
    (Hamelle)   1876-1879
L'Amour et le Crane—Baudelaire (Schott)   1884
Chansons Populaires (Heugel)   1892
Lied Maritime—Vincent d'Indy (Rouart-Lerolle) 1896

Les Noces d'Or du Sacerdoce—Delaporte (Schola
　Cantorum)　　　　　　　　　　　　　　　　　1898

La Première Dent—Laurencie (Durand)　　　　1898

Mirages—Paul Gravolet (Hamelle)　　　　　　1903

Les Yeux de l'Aimée—Vincent d'Indy (Gramo-
　phone Michaelis, Milan)　　　　　　　　　　1904

Vocalise (Leduc)　　　　　　　　　　　　　　1907

Madrigal pour Soprano et Violoncelle (Heugel)　1928

VOCAL ENSEMBLE

La Chanson des Adventuriers de la Mer—Hugo
　(Schott)　　　　　　　　　　　　　　　　　1870
　　　(Baryton, Chœur et Piano)

Cantate Domino (Durand)　　　　　　　　　　1885
　　　(Trois Voix avec Orgues)

Sainte Marie-Madeleine (Durand)　　　　　　1885
　　　(Soprano, Chœur de Femmes, Piano et
　　　　Harmonium)

Sur la Mer—Vincent d'Indy (Hamelle)　　　　1888
　　　(Chœur de Femmes)

" L'Art et le Peuple " (Hamelle)　　　　　　1894
　　　(Quatre Voix d'Hommes)

Motet—" Deus Israel " (Schola Cantorum)　　1896
　　　(Quatre Voix mixtes)

Motet—" Sancta　Maria,　succurre　miseris "
　(Schola Cantorum)　　　　　　　　　　　　1898
　　　(Deux Voix égales)

" O Gai Soleil " (La Révue Musicale)　　　　1909
　　　(Chœur et canon à deux Voix)

Vingt-quatres Cantiques Populaires Grégorienné
　—" Pentecosten " (Schola Cantorum)　　　　1919

Motet—"Ave, Regina Coelorum " (Schola Can-
　torum)　　　　　　　　　　　　　　　　　1922
　　　(Quatre Voix mixtes)

Trois Chansons Populaires Françaises (Rouart-
   Lerolle)   1924
     (Chœur sans accompagnement)
        1. Querelle d'Amour
        2. Histoire de jeune Soldat
        3. Lisette
Deux Motets en honneur de la canonisation de
   Saint Jean Eudes (Schola Cantorum)   1925
Motet—" O Domine mea " (Schola Cantorum) 1926
   (Deux Voix égales)
Six Chants Populaires Français (Rouart-Lerolle) 1927
   (Chœur sans accompagnement)
Le Bouquet de Printemps (Rouart-Lerolle)   1928
   (Trois Voix égales sans accompagnement)
" Les Trois Fileuses " (Billaudot)   1929
   (Trois Voix égales)
Six Chants Populaires Français (2e recueil)
   (Durand)   1930

SOPRANO AND ORCHESTRA

" Clair de Lune "—Victor Hugo (Hamelle)   1872-1881
Six Chansons Anciennes du Vivarais (Deux
   Recueils)   1926 and 1930
Cent Thèmes d'Harmonie et Réalisations (Roud-
   anez)   1907-1918

ORGAN

Prélude et Petit Canon (Durand)   1893
Vêpres du Commun des Martyrs (Schola Can-
   torum)   1899
Pièce en mi bémol (Durand)   1911

MILITARY BAND

March du 76e Régiment d'Infanterie (Durand)   1903

THEATRE MUSIC

" Karadec " (Heugel)   1890
" Medée " (Durand)   1898

EDITIONS

" Orfeo " (Monteverde)   Schola Cantorum
" L'incoronazione di Poppea " (Monte-
    verde)   Schola Cantorum
" Les Eléments " (Destouches)   Michaelis
" Dardanus " (Rameau)   Durand
" Hippolyte et Aricie " (Rameau)   Durand
" Naïs " (Rameau)   Durand
Sonatas (Rust)   Rouart-Lerolle

APPENDIX B

LITERARY WORKS

I HAVE omitted the numerous articles which d'Indy wrote
for the Press and for musical journals as they are unobtain-
able in book form.

Cours de Composition musicale (Durand)

Volume 1	Published	1903
Volume 2		
Part One	,,	1909
Part Two	,,	1933
Volume 3	,,	1950

César Franck (" Maîtres de Musique ", Alcan)   1906
César Franck (Trans. Rosa Newmarch, The Bodley
    Head)   1909
Beethoven (Laurens)   1911
Richard Wagner (Delagrave)   1930

APPENDIX C

BIBLIOGRAPHY

THIS list consists of useful and easily available books and articles. Numerous studies of d'Indy have appeared in journals, but for the most part they are difficult or impossible to find. I have made exceptions in the case of two books which, although out of print, may possibly be picked up in second-hand bookshops and bookstalls in France. These are:

Les Idées de M. Vincent d'Indy Saint-Saëns
Vincent d'Indy   Jean de la Laurencie

Although back numbers of *Le Revue Musicale* are out of print also, the bookshops on the Boul' Mich, Paris, seem to stock a good many of them. Attention should be drawn, therefore, to the following *numéros spéciales* of this journal:

" Vincent d'Indy "   January 1932
  Vincent d'Indy—Henri Prunières
  Sur Vincent d'Indy—Paul Dukas
  L'Oeuvre de piano de Vincent d'Indy—Alfred Cortot
  Le classe de d'Indy au Conservatoire—Arthur
    Honegger

"Autour de Vincent d'Indy " August-September 1937
  Le Theatre lyrique de Vincent d'Indy—Gustave
    Samazeuilh
  Souvenirs homériques: Vincent d'Indy, auteur
    d'operette—Xavier de Courville
  Vincent d'Indy et son temps—Arthur Hoerée

and to certain numbers containing isolated articles of particular interest. These are:

September 1946
La Mélodie de Vincent d'Indy—Léon Vallas

October 1946

La Mélodie de Vincent d'Indy: Réponse à Leon Vallas—
Guy de Lioncourt

February 1947

Lettres inédites de Saint-Saëns et de Vincent d'Indy,
commentées par Léon Vallas

Books easily obtainable from France include:

Vincent d'Indy	Louis Borgex
Vincent d'Indy	J. Canteloube
Vincent d'Indy (two volumes)	Léon Vallas
Le Schola Cantorum en 1925	Vincent d'Indy et Autres
Musiciens d'Aujourd'hui	Romain Rolland
La Musique contemporaine en France (two volumes)	René Dumesnil
La Musique en France entre les deux guerres	René Dumesnil
Histoire Illustrée de la Musique	René Dumesnil
La Musique Française de Franck à Debussy	Paul Landormy
La Musique Française apres Debussy	Paul Landormy
Ecrits sur la Musique	Paul Dukas
De Rameau à Ravel	Pierre Lalo
Musiciens de mon temps	Gustave Samazeuilh

Books and articles in English include:

Musicians of To-day	Romain Rolland
French Music of To-day	Jean Aubry
Article in *Grove's Dictionary*	Léon Vallas
Article in *Cyclopaedic Survey of Chamber Music*	M. D. Calvocoressi
Article in *Music Survey*, March 1950	Norman Demuth

At the time of going to press, articles are scheduled to
appear in many musical journals during the Centenary Year.

INDEX TO MUSICAL EXAMPLES

GENERAL INDEX

SOME TRENDS
OF 20TH CENTURY MUSIC
BY NORMAN DEMUTH

Professor Demuth's new book is a study of certain composers who may justly be said to have played an important part in the history of world music and who, consequently, have arrived at a state of maturity and have already influenced the trend of future music. They have formulated certain facets of twentieth-century music and have become representative of the first half of the century. Some are giants, others have played a great part within the limits of their own cultures without, perhaps, making a direct world impact.

There are twenty-seven chapters in all, the titles of which are given below.

CONTENTS

Over 130 music illustrations

APPROX. 35s. NET